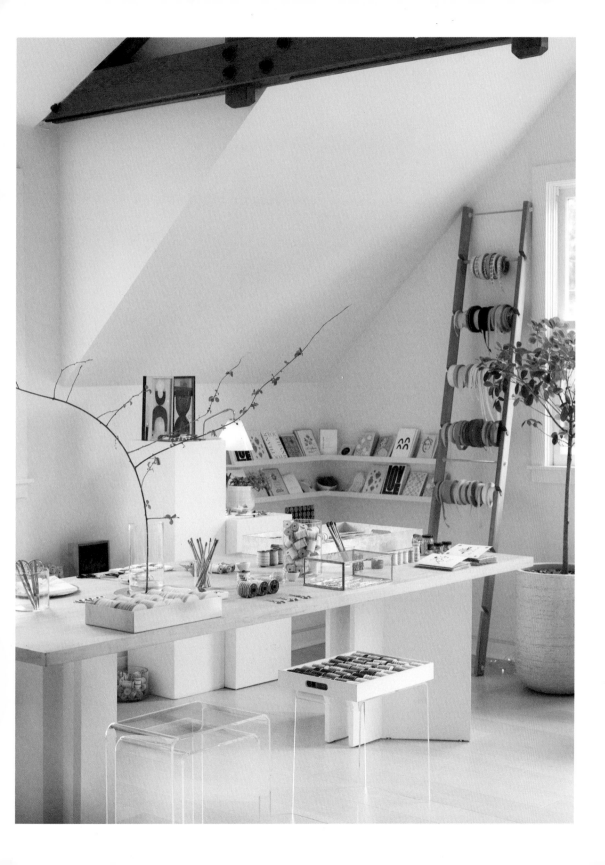

THE RIBBON STUDIO

INSPIRING GIFTS AND CRAFT PROJECTS FOR EVERY OCCASION

FROM ANGELA LIGUORI AND STUDIO CARTA

TEXT AND PROJECT DESIGNS BY
COCO MCCRACKEN, LAURA MURPHY, AND SILKE STODDARD

PRINCIPAL PHOTOGRAPHY BY DANE TASHIMA
PRODUCED BY JAN HARTMAN BOOKS

ABRAMS, NEW YORK

To my parents, who always supported my creativity, and to my husband and our three children, who inspire everything I do!

Editor: Shawna Mullen
Designer: Brooke Reynolds for inchmark
Design Manager: Jenice Kim
Managing Editor: Logan Hill
Production Manager: Kathleen Gaffney

Library of Congress Control Number: 2024935809

ISBN: 978-1-4197-7288-7
eISBN: 979-8-88707-250-0

Text copyright © 2024 Studio Carta
See page 175 for photography credits

Cover © 2024 Abrams

Printed and bound in China
10 9 8 7 6 5 4 3 2 1

Abrams books are available at special discounts when purchased in quantity for premiums and promotions as well as fundraising or educational use. Special editions can also be created to specification. For details, contact specialsales@abramsbooks.com or the address below.

Abrams® is a registered trademark of Harry N. Abrams, Inc.

ABRAMS The Art of Books
195 Broadway, New York, NY 10007
abramsbooks.com

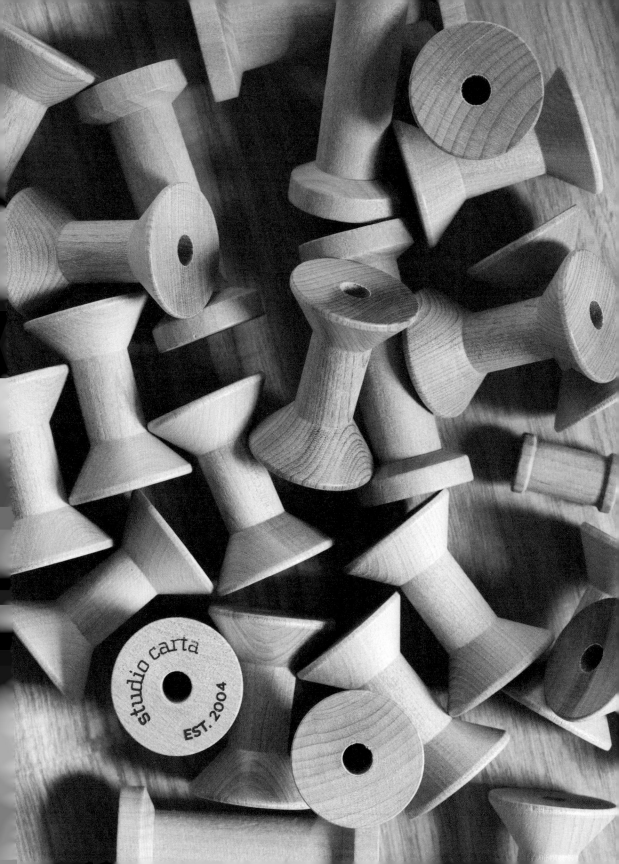

CONTENTS

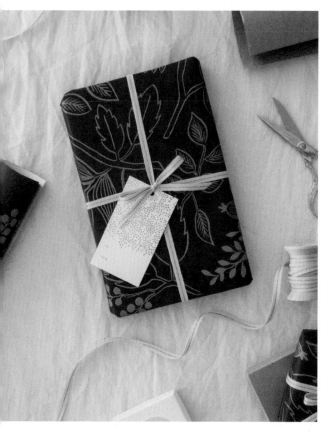

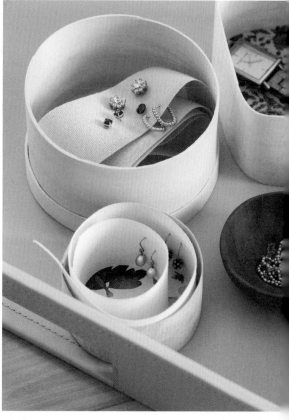

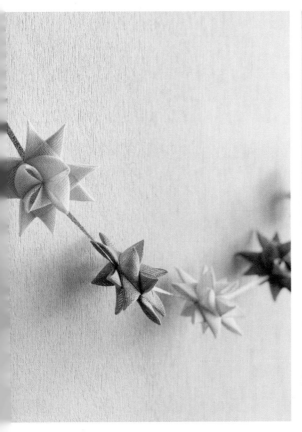
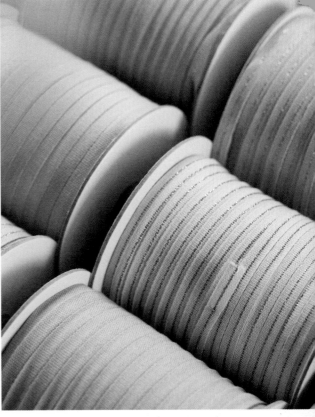

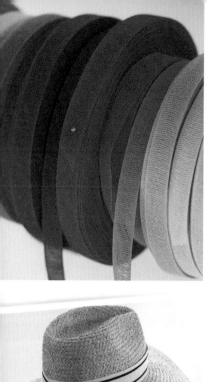
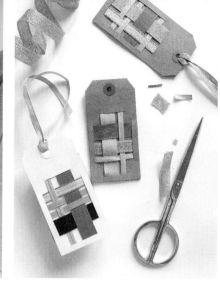
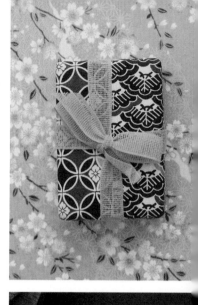
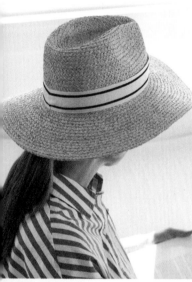
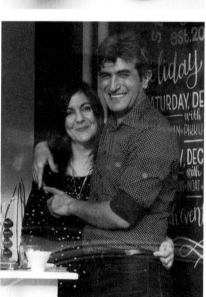
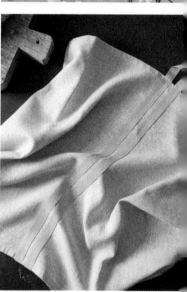
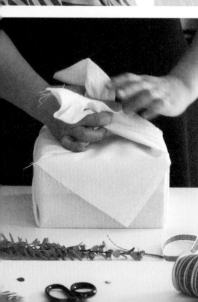
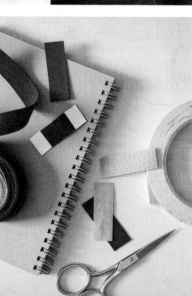
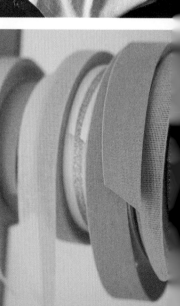

FOREWORD

I first met Angela Liguori more than a decade ago when I spotted her and Studio Carta ribbons across a crowded room at the Gift Show in New York City. Her booth stood out in a sea of a thousand vendors; the colors and quality of her ribbons made for the most beautiful display.

From then on, I looked out to see what Studio Carta had that was new. I loved choosing ribbons as the perfect finishing touches for my projects, first as the editorial director of *Martha Stewart Weddings*, then when I was writing *Celebrate Everything*, and now for my business as the Celebration Expert, helping people dream up unforgettable celebrations.

The beauty and joy in celebrations are in the details. This book demonstrates that Angela's Studio Carta ribbons are details that might just steal the whole show. They make bridal bouquets even more beautiful, adding elegance and anticipation to wrapped presents or gift boxes. I even have a glass jar filled with Studio Carta ribbons on display in my studio because I love using them in projects and looking at them to inspire color palettes for celebrations, floral displays, favor packaging, product designs, and more.

This stunning book showcases that tying bouquets and encircling packages is just the beginning of what ribbons can do. It leads the reader through step-by-step projects using ribbons to make everything from practical and pretty shoelaces to ribbon flower garlands and bouquets that last forever. Beautiful and sustainable, Studio Carta ribbons are treasures that you can use again and again—and *The Ribbon Studio* explains how to make them last even longer.

—Darcy Miller,
Celebration Expert and founder of Darcy Miller Designs

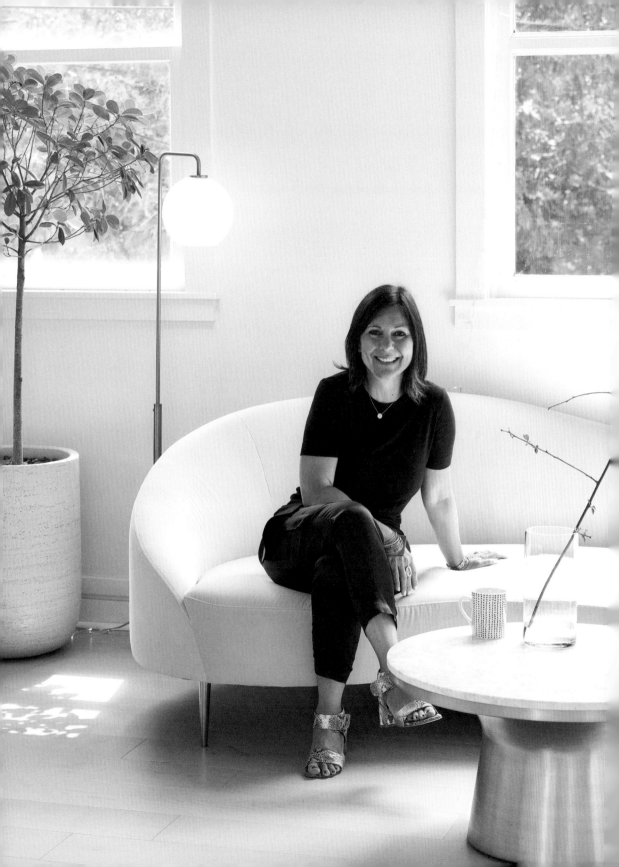

INTRODUCTION

THE CREATIVE POWER OF RIBBON

Behold the power of ribbon. Sturdy, flexible, and in colors that delight. As crafters, it's the ribbon we find ourselves always reaching for. It is appealing due to its high-quality nature and the fact that it is cotton, available in varying widths and weaves, lending itself to an array of uses. As we hope you will find on the following pages, this ribbon transcends gift wrap—it is *special.* It's a material you can use in a practical, utilitarian way (making a tea towel more functional, for example) or for pure pleasure (making something more beautiful, like happy replacements for basic shoelaces). Even a few inches of ribbon can be saved for a rainy day, coveted, kept, or displayed. It can come in handy around the house or provide the finishing touch on a special gift for someone you love.

The aim of this book is to illustrate the unlimited projects that can abound when crafting with ribbon. It also will inspire your own ribbon creations and highlight the passion and creativity of so many crafters and artists who share a connection with the world of ribbon and Studio Carta.

To shop ribbon, and for more inspiration on how to use it, head to www.studiocartashop.com.

Angela Liguori in the Studio Carta studio in Chestnut Hill, Massachusetts.

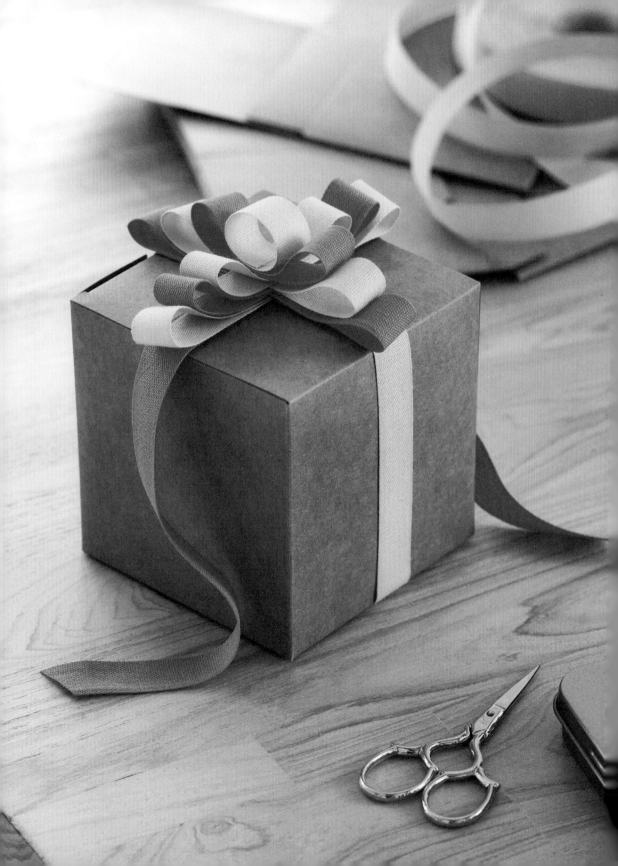

CREATIVE WRAPPING IDEAS

TASSELS

Create stunning tassels using ribbon that is ¼ inch (6 mm) wide and thread.

1

SUPPLIES

Scissors

Ribbon, ¼ inch (6 mm) wide

Gold thread

Gift box

ONE Cut eight to ten pieces of ribbon to 6 inches (15 cm).

TWO Center them on top of a 12-inch (30.5 cm) length of gold thread and tie. (Pull the thread as tight as you can so the ribbons cinch!)

THREE Fold in half and pinch together at top. Cut another 12-inch (30.5 cm) length of gold thread and start wrapping around all ribbons, about ½ to ¾ inches (1.3 to 2 cm) from top. Wrap, wrap, wrap! Then tie with a double knot and trim the ends.

Affix to another ribbon for wrapping, or use the thread already attached to the tassel to tie to a package.

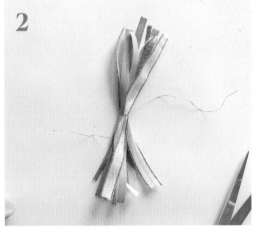

2

3

IMAGINE!

Let your imagination run wild to create unique and original gift wraps.

ONE Wrapping paper by British designer Katie Leamon offers inspiration for using beautiful paper in combination with wide or thin cotton ribbon and greenery.

TWO Selecting a wide ribbon for this square box offers the perfect complement to the modern graphic of this paper. Tie it all together with a bow.

THREE Alternatively, choose a simple, light gift paper and matching ribbon adorned with a sprig of holiday greenery.

Your choice of paper, ribbon, and greenery is everything to creating a gorgeous and individual statement.

KNOTTED RIBBONS

What to do with those remnant ribbon pieces that can't quite wrap around a whole package? Transform a plain package into a colorful display of leftover ribbon pieces. The result is a fireworks burst of ribbons, set off against a solid landscape of wrapping paper.

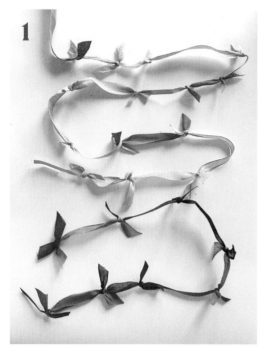

ONE Simply use a square knot to tie your ribbon sections together, allowing for about an inch at either end.

TWO Keep going . . . and going! Trim ends at an angle.

THREE Wrap your packages with your very own unique ribbon! Beautiful!

FUROSHIKI

Those looking for a chic and sustainable alternative to rolls of paper wrap might consider the centuries-old tradition of *furoshiki*. This traditional Japanese cloth wrapping is a very special (and practical) way to wrap gifts, culinary treats, and flowers. Furoshiki often features thicker, square-shaped decorative fabrics, hemmed edges, and hand-painted designs to personalize your gift.

ONE Wrap up with a self-tie or ribbon bowtie; add a sprig of sage, rosemary, or holiday green.

TWO A wrapping of cotton, linen, silk, or other materials means the cloth can be used for other practical purposes, such as a tea towel or napkin.

THREE In our project, we've wrapped a bouquet of common though beautiful garden flowers and greens in a furoshiki cloth to create a very special gift.

Furoshiki gifts come in a variety of sizes, though usually square and decorated with a sprig of nature, such as eucalyptus or evergreen.

A FUROSHIKI GIFT

This Japanese tradition offers endless possibilities for the cloth wrap, complementary ribbons, and nature's found decor.

ONE A simple tie on top binds together the two sides of the fabric.

TWO Your tie should look like this.

THREE Trim the edges and add a sprig of local greenery to the top.

WOVEN TAGS

Weave ribbon in different colors and gauges together and voila! Mini masterpieces on top of packages, on tags, on envelopes—you name it!

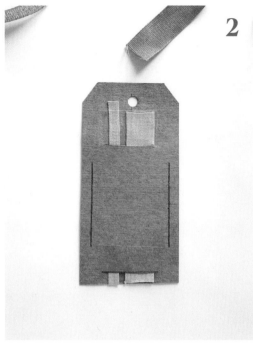

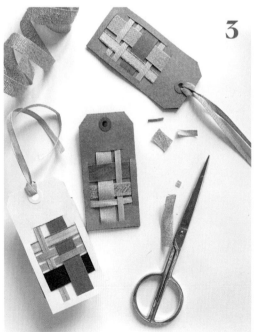

SUPPLIES

Craft knife

Blank tags or envelopes

Ribbon

Double-sided tape

ONE Start by using a craft knife, cut four 2-inch (5 cm) slits about ¼ inch (6 mm) from the edges of your tag.

TWO Then, tuck ribbon of your choice through the slits vertically and tape to secure.

THREE Next, weave ribbon of your choice through horizontally—over, under. Trim and tape to secure. Finish by using double-sided tape or paste to adhere a blank tag on top of the back of your woven masterpiece to create a clean backing.

RIBBON WREATHS

Save your ribbon scraps to create these sweet gift toppers.

1

2

3

SUPPLIES

About fifteen pieces of ribbon, 2 inches (5 cm) long

1-inch (2.5 cm) paper circle

Clear glue

Gift box

Stamped or written letter

ONE Glue first piece of 2-inch (5 cm) ribbon to the center of the paper circle.

TWO Begin overlapping and layering ribbon in a circular motion until wreath is complete.

THREE Add a dot of glue between each piece. Personalize with a stamped or written letter and adhere to top of gift box, as shown left.

MIDNIGHT
AND SHIMMER

Ah, the drama of nature! Add a pinecone, a sprig of holly, or a berry bud to your midnight black paper and metallic colored ribbon—a dramatic display of nature, night, and cotton!

The possibilities are unlimited with narrow and wide ribbons and nature's bounty. Here, the black paper is a striking background for the braided metallic and the loose weave metallic ribbon.

RIBBON TREE GIFT TOPPER

Make shapes with ribbon, like this festive tree, no taping or gluing required!

1

2

3

SUPPLIES

Thin thread, string, or ribbon for anchoring

Wrapped package

Ribbon

ONE Create your anchor by tying thinner ribbon, thread, or twine once around your wrapped package. (If making a tree, have one section tied lower on the package versus right around the center.)

TWO Tuck one end of ribbon under the anchor at the top of your package. Begin weaving ribbon in larger and larger "loops" as you make your way down.

THREE Continue to use the center ribbon as an anchor. At the bottom of the package, leave a pretty ribbon tail as shown and finish by cutting the tail at an angle.

SPARKLE PLENTY

Nothing says happiness and friendship like beautiful and thoughtful gift wrapping. The gift wrap is part of the gift itself!

SUPPLIES

1 wide ribbon, long enough to wrap around the package's width and length

1 narrower ribbon in a complementary or contrasting color

1 piece of gift paper to wrap package

This wonderfully stylish way to impress your friends and family can be created from beautiful gift paper found in specialty paper and craft shops and complementary glittery ribbons, one wide, one narrower.

BOOK STACKS

Create beautiful stacks of books or wrapped packages with intertwined, layered ribbon. The possibilities are endless!

1

2

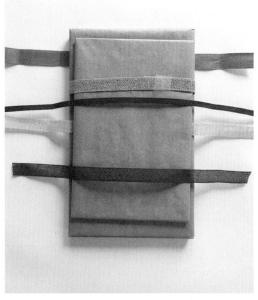

3

SUPPLIES

Ribbon at least twice the length and height of the package you are wrapping, per ribbon

Books or wrapped packages

Tape

Scissors

ONE Lay a few pieces of ribbon on a flat surface, and begin by stacking one book or package on top.

TWO Tape to secure. Repeat for as many packages or books as you'd like, layering and taping as you go.

THREE Wrap one wider ribbon around the entire stack to secure.

Keep layering ribbon! Simply choose your ribbons to layer and tape to secure at the back.

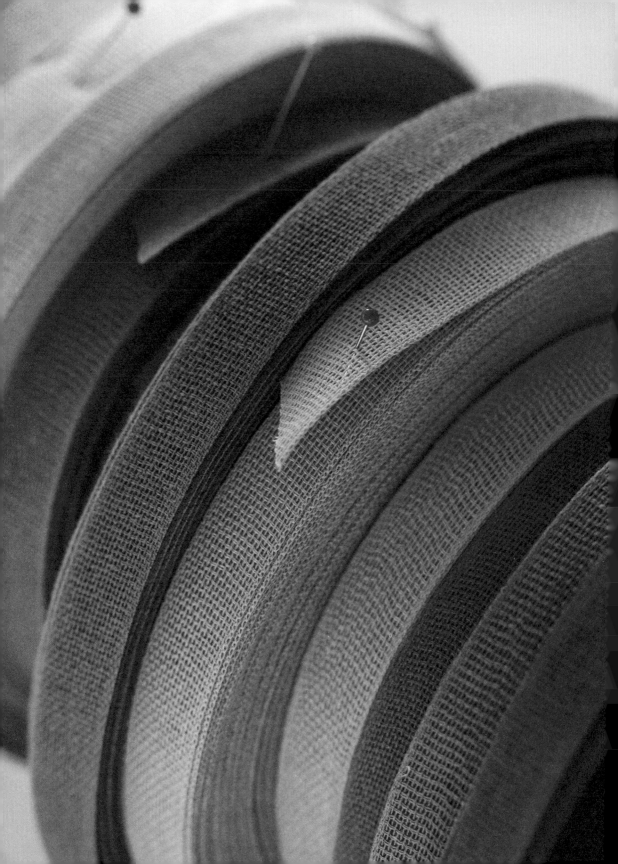

RIBBON DIYS GIFTS & KEEPSAKES

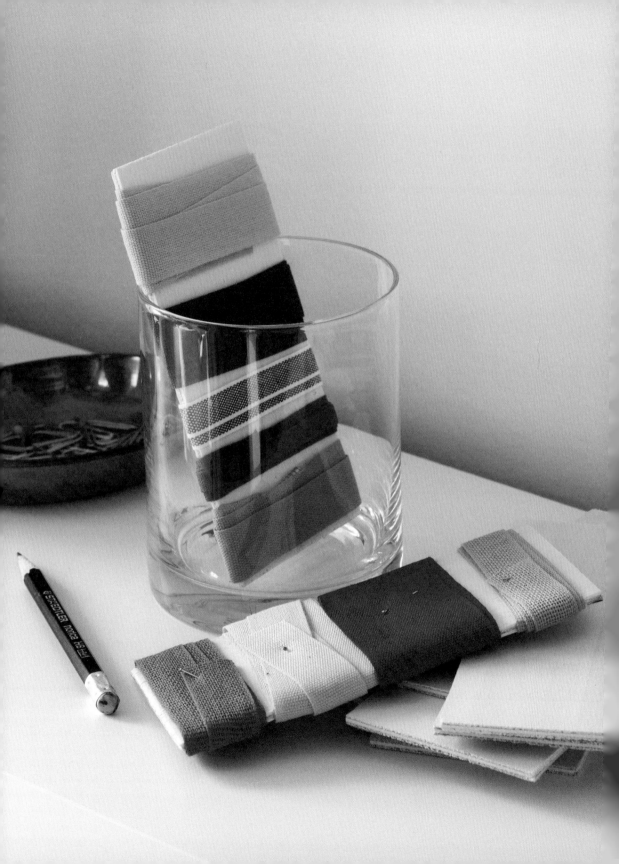

RIBBON BASICS

Master the basics for storing, using, and preserving ribbon, then try your hand at the dozen clever ribbon projects that follow. You can make unique gifts and pretty treasures to keep or share.

HOW TO STORE RIBBON AT HOME

At Studio Carta, yards and yards of ribbon live on various spools, either stacked or hanging off dowels. But in our own craft spaces at home, we'll often have shorter lengths of ribbon: Perhaps they were once wrapped around a gift or left over from a project. These are worthy of storing for future projects; in fact, many of the projects on the pages that follow are meant to give new life to leftovers.

You could amass pieces of ribbon in your ribbon box and pull them out when inspiration strikes, ironing them back to life (see below). We like to organize them from the start, which is both practical and a beautiful way to display your stash. Organize the ribbons by kind, by width, and/or by color. Seeing your ribbon might inspire new projects—your own little ribbon studio at home.

To store on balsa wood, as pictured, make sure the ribbon is flat. (Iron them first as explained below if needed.)

Use a piece of balsa wood 2 to 3 inches (5 to 7.5 cm) wide. Tape the end of your ribbon length to the wood and start wrapping the ribbon until you've reached the end. If you have more than about 1 yard (91 cm), you'll want the ribbon to slightly overlap with each winding, so it doesn't get too thick and "fall off."

When you get to the end, use a short pin to pierce the layers below, holding the ribbon in place.

AT RIGHT

There are wood spools for sale at many online suppliers. Wrap each of your ribbon lengths around a separate spool—again, keeping them flat—and secure with a pin. Then thread a piece of thin ribbon or twine through the spools and hang them together. This also makes for a great storage solution for washi tape.

ABOVE If you're lucky enough to have a few yards of the same ribbon, you can wrap it around itself using your hand. Take one end of your ribbon length and drape it around your index finger. Hold the end in place with your thumb, then wrap the ribbon around all four fingers until you get to the end. Gently slide the bundle off your fingers and tie together with one of the tiny pieces you're keeping in your basket (see following spread).

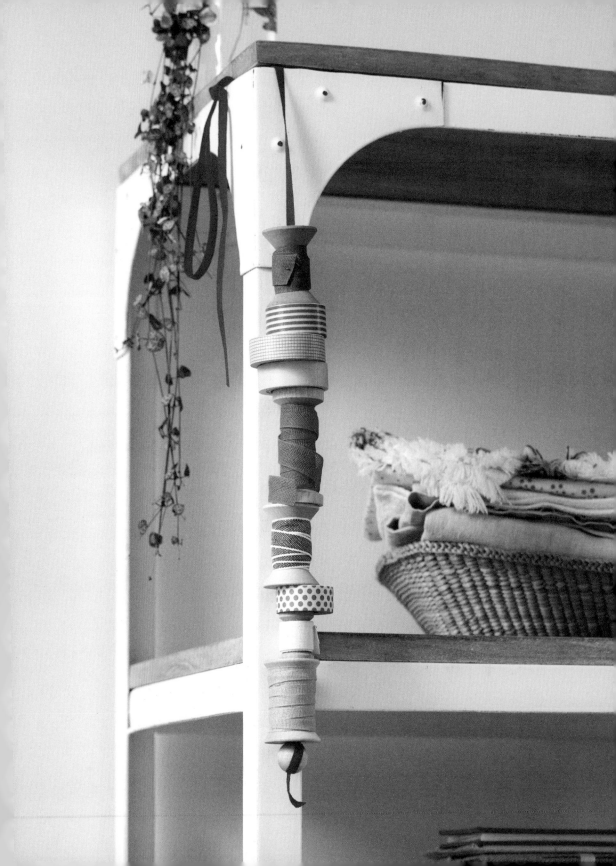

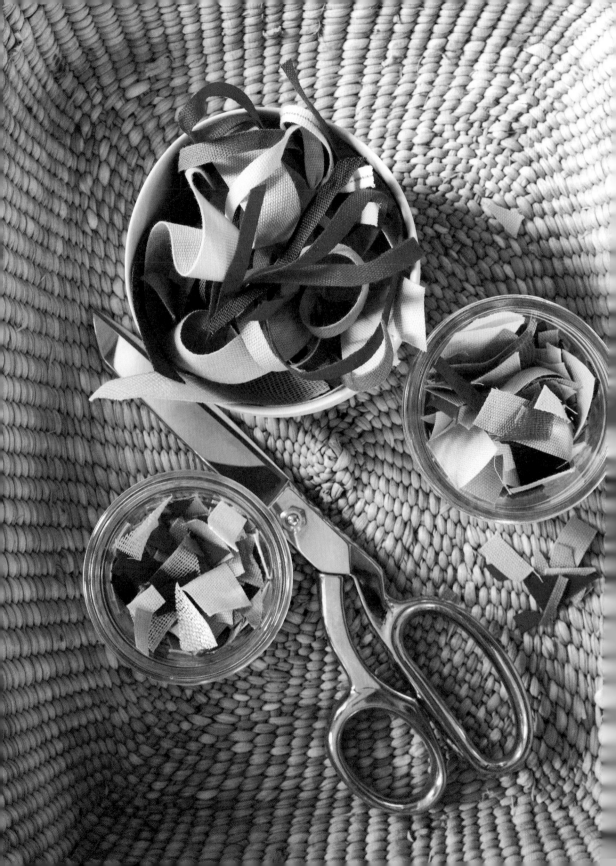

AT LEFT

No piece of ribbon is too short to keep. If you have pieces that are not long enough to wind, just nestle them together nicely in a basket. And even the tiniest bits of ribbon have a use: DIY confetti. How fun to sneak inside a birthday card, or to shower bits of color on your tablescape. Simply collect your tiniest pieces in small glass jars.

HOW TO REVIVE RIBBON

You can reuse ribbon multiple times, so no need to throw it away with the gift wrap. (Save your gift wrap, too!) Using a regular iron, you can make your ribbon look like new. Make sure you set the heat according to the material of your ribbon; for Studio Carta's ribbon, the cotton setting works well. Place your ribbon on an ironing board, hold the iron on top, and pull the ribbon underneath the iron toward you. Repeat if it is very wrinkled. Once flat, store using one of the methods mentioned above.

HOW TO CARE FOR RIBBON

Studio Carta ribbons were made for bookbinding, and therefore they don't go through the usual scrutiny of materials meant for washing. That doesn't have to prevent you from using them for some projects that might need to be washed, as long as you're aware that they might shrink slightly or the color may fade.

When sewing the ribbons onto another textile, make sure you prewash both materials first. Prewashing entails soaking the ribbon in warm water for an hour or so, hanging to dry, and then pressing flat with a hot iron.

When mixing various ribbons for projects (the coaster project on page 81 being a good example), the piece might shrink a little, just like anything made from cotton would. Some colors tend to bleed more than others, so be mindful when combining colors for projects you intend to wash. To test for color fastness, soak a swatch of the ribbon you want to use in warm water along with a piece of white cloth. If the color of the water changes or the color transfers to the white cloth after a few hours of soaking, the ribbon is not color fast.

When sewing a longer length of ribbon, first stretch the ribbon a little to ease the selvedge. When it comes off the roll, it might bow a little to one side. Stretching the ribbon and ironing it before stitching it will help to straighten.

AT RIGHT

To personalize your scissors (or to color-code them by use), add a short length of ribbon around the handle.

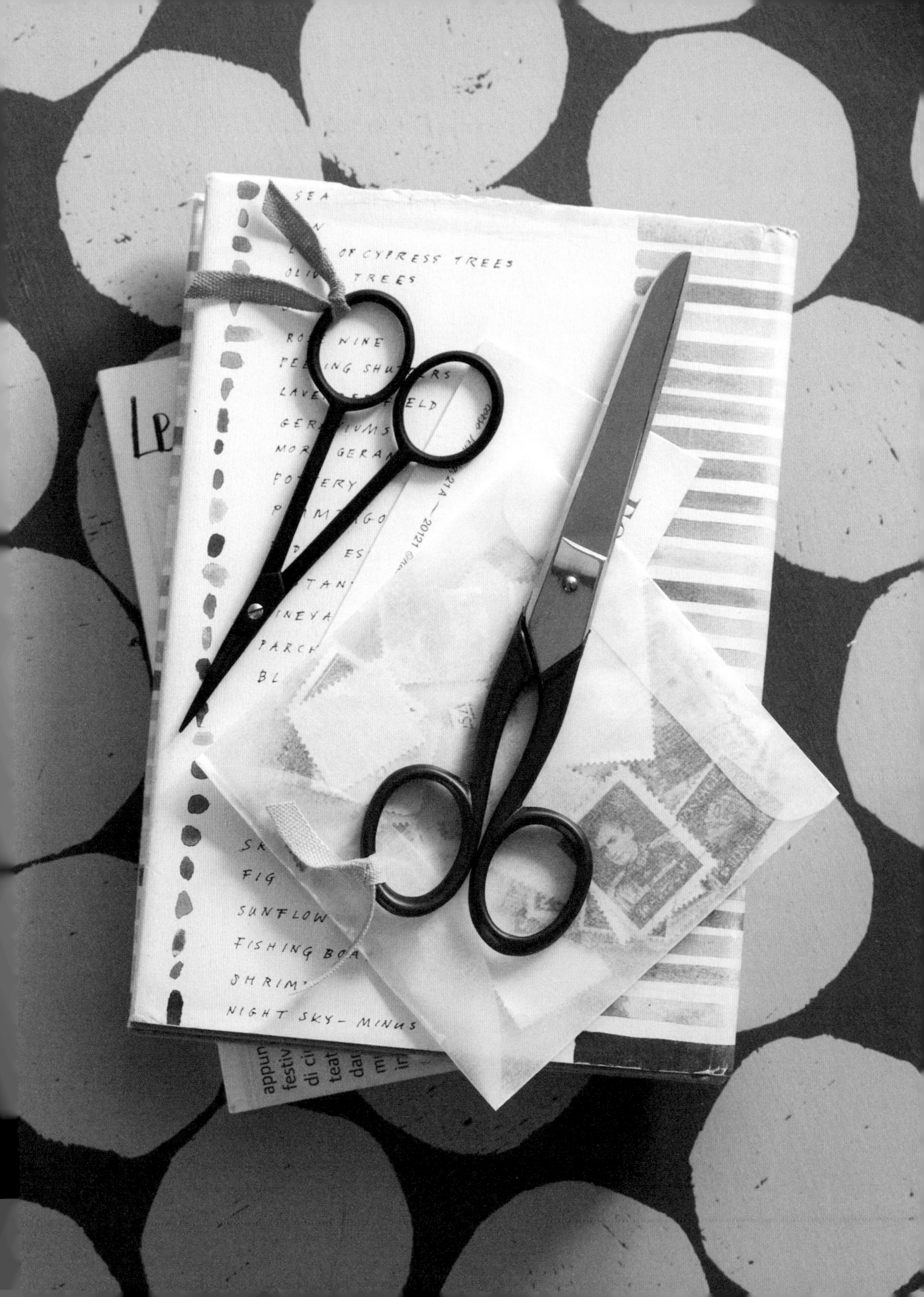
SEA
OF CYPRESS TREES
TREES
FIG
NIGHT SKY- MINUS

HOW TO PREVENT RIBBON FROM FRAYING

As far as we're concerned, fraying adds character. But for some projects, especially ones that are meant to last or get a lot of use, giving the end cut of your ribbon a seal to avoid fraying will be helpful. There are many products out in the sewing world that are made specifically for stopping fabrics (and ribbons) from fraying. If you already own those, feel free to use them at the end of a piece of freshly cut ribbon.

Or, make your own. Because those products are really just watered down craft glue, you can use a teaspoon of glue and slowly incorporate drops of water. Stir the glue with a toothpick, until it has the consistency of heavy cream. Use a small brush with short, stiff bristles and dab this glue mix onto the ribbon end. The less you use, the less visible it will be. Allow time for drying and craft away.

You can do the same with clear nail polish, which is great for projects that might get wet (the coaster project being a good example). Just use the brush that already comes with the bottle and dab it onto the ribbon in tiny amounts, all across the cut end. Allow time for drying.

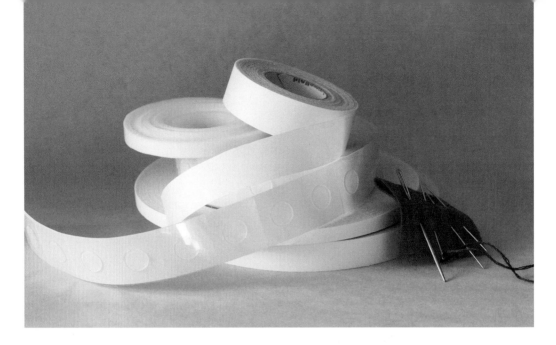

HOW TO ADHERE RIBBON TO OTHER MATERIALS

One of the goals of this book is to illustrate how universal ribbon can be; they're not just used for wrapping. Studio Carta ribbons are made with cotton, which lends itself to all sorts of applications, like embellishing other textiles such as pillows or curtains (in which case you'd want to sew them on, either by hand or using a machine). You can use regular sewing thread in a matching color. Or, if you want your stitches more pronounced in your hand sewing, you can use embroidery floss (just use half the threads). Positioning tape is very helpful if you want to make sure your ribbon stays in place when sewing and you don't want to have to sew over pins (an example being the pincushion project on page 87). Plain painter's tape works in some cases too (an example being the coaster project on page 81).

If using positioning tape, just adhere the tape to your ribbon, peel off the paper, and position it to your textile. Then stitch in place. The tape will wash away in the first washing (or just stay hidden, which is fine). For projects that aren't meant to be washed, or if you just want a quick fix, there is fusible tape (often called "hem tape"). Place the tape on the back of your ribbon and iron on. Remove the paper, place the ribbon on your textile (or even paper, if you're making a card), and iron once more.

If you want to attach ribbon to paper instead of fabric (like for our notebook project on page 61), you can use a strong, non-removable, double-sided tape. Choose the same width tape as the ribbon you'll use, adhere to your ribbon, remove the protective film, and press onto your paper or card.

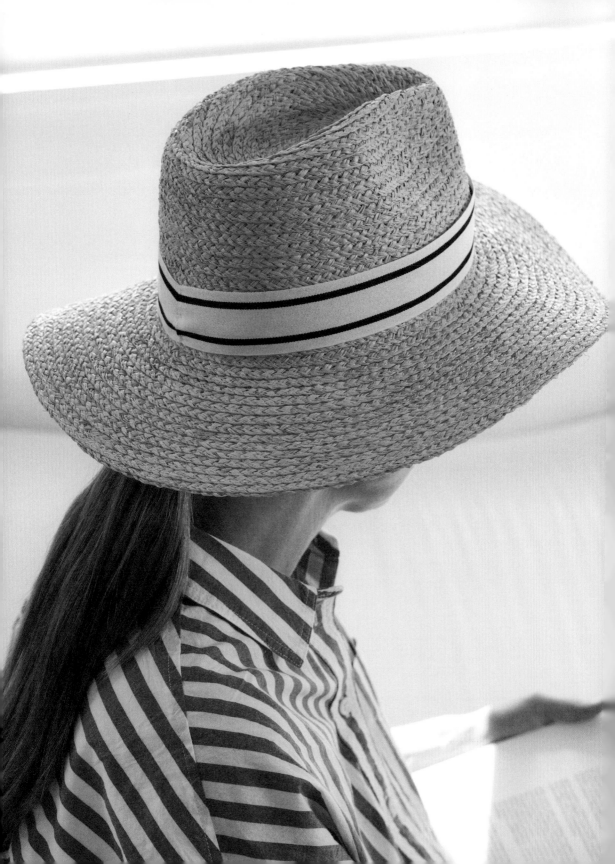

Ribbon Hat Band

Dress up a favorite summer hat by adding a wide ribbon band. Swap it out for a different ribbon when the mood strikes!

SUPPLIES

Tight weave cotton ribbon, 1½ inches (4 cm) wide and measured ½ inch (1.3 cm) longer than the circumference of your hat (pictured in the colors Natural and Black)

Sewing needle and thread

Scissors

Note: We found that hats with a tall and flat crown work best.

You can also use ribbon to create straps by stitching two lengths of ribbon to the inside of the hat; tie at neck.

Apply both techniques to children's hats (supplying straps for little ones who are inclined to pull hats off!).

ONE Adhere ribbon end to hat by first folding ¼ inch (6 mm) of the ribbon's end underneath itself. Attach one stitch at the center of the ribbon. Knot to secure the stitch on the inside and snip ends.

TWO Holding the ribbon tightly against the hat, begin wrapping the ribbon around the hat brim, keeping the ribbon as flat as possible. Apply a stitch every 6 to 8 inches (15 to 20 cm).

THREE Once you have worked all the way around the hat, fold the end of the ribbon under ¼ inch (6 mm) once again to create a clean seam. Apply three small stitches—one at the top of the ribbon end, one in the middle, and one at the bottom—to complete.

Odds and Ends

Tight weave ribbon makes snug storage for earrings and other odds and ends while on the go. This makes for a great packaging hack when gifting jewelry inside a small box.

SUPPLIES

Any leftover ribbon piece—preferably tight weave cotton ribbon, 1½ inch (4 cm) wide (pictured in the color Blush)

Pierce earrings and brooches through any piece of tight weave ribbon you have around (or slip a hair clip or pin on there as well). Roll ribbon and store, or slip into a pouch for travel or for taking your odds-and-ends on the go.

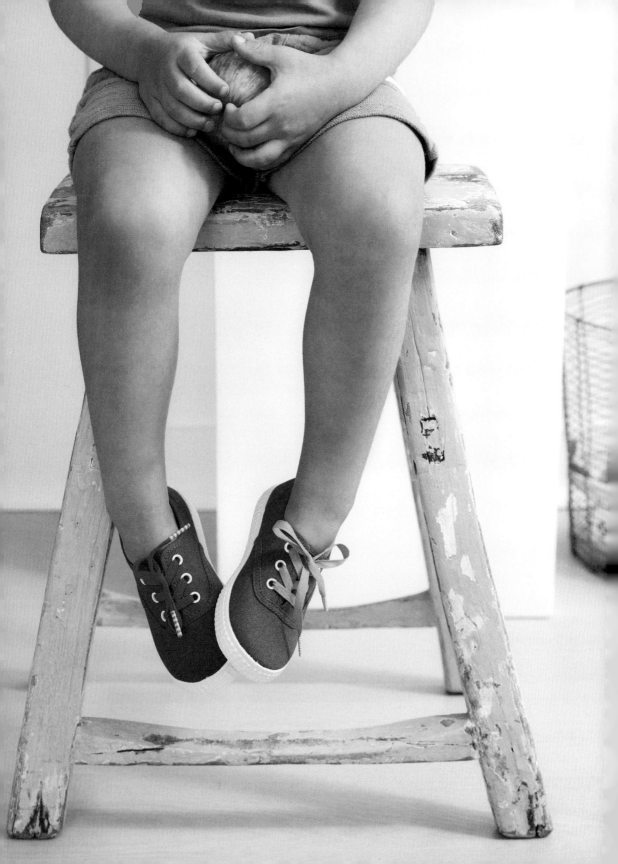

Colorful Laces

Swap out existing laces for vibrant colored ribbons in this sweet shoe upgrade. Here, washi tape serves as a DIY aglet, which provides a polished look for the ends of your laces while keeping them in place.

SUPPLIES

Measuring tape

Scissors

Tight weave ribbon, ¼ inch (6 mm) wide (pictured in the colors Pool, Lemon, Red, and Melon). This project calls for about 24 to 36 inches (61 to 91 cm) of ribbon, but use the original lace length as a guide for trimming ribbon length.

Washi tape

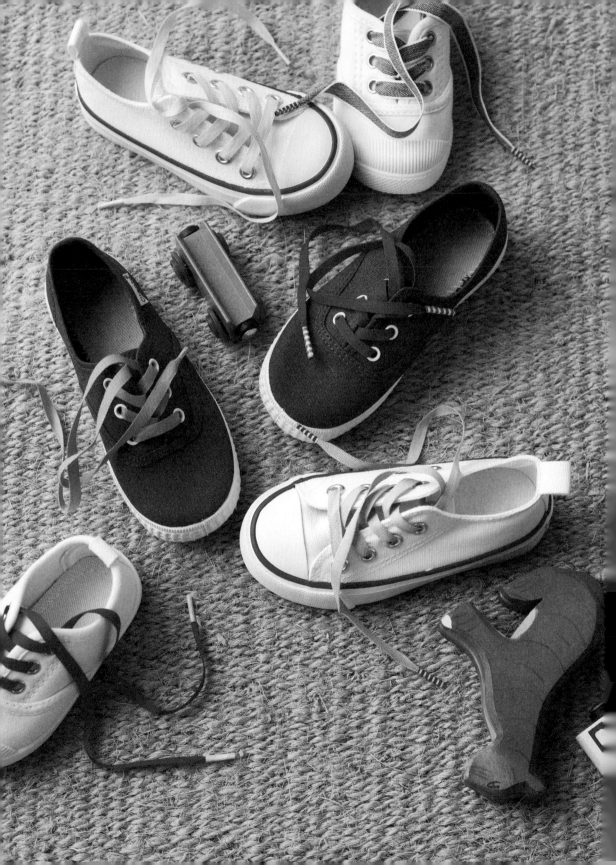

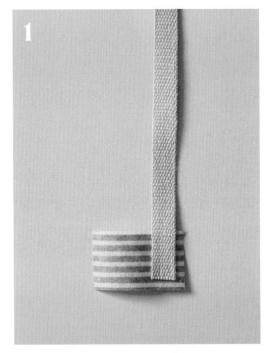

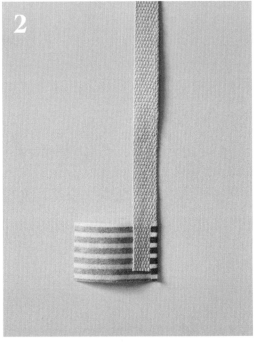

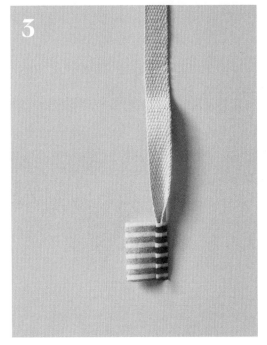

Remove existing laces from shoes and measure their length. Cut two pieces of ribbon to match lace length.

ONE Cut a 1-inch (2.5 cm) piece of washi tape and lay on a flat surface widthwise. Place one end of the ribbon on top of the washi tape, allowing for a ⅛-inch (3 mm) margin from both edges of the tape.

TWO Fold the ⅛-inch (3 mm) piece of exposed tape onto the ribbon edge.

THREE Slowly roll the tape around the ribbon, ensuring it stays as tight as possible until you reach the end of the tape.

Repeat for the other lace.

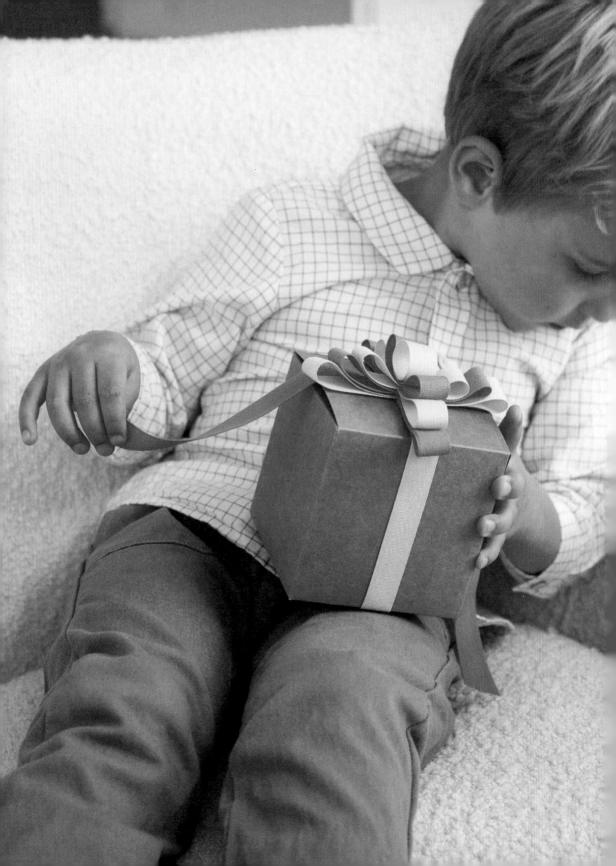

Unexpected Gift Wrap

This is not your average bow. Layered ribbon loops are all you need to make a statement atop simple packaging. Add or remove layers and mix up the colors. Happy wrapping!

SUPPLIES

Scissors

Tight weave cotton ribbon, ⅝ inch (1.5 cm) wide. This project calls for 41 inches (105 cm) of ribbon in one color (pictured in the color Melon) and 44 inches (112 cm) of ribbon in a second color (pictured in the color Blush).

Adhesive dots measuring 0.3 inch (8 mm)

Gift box. The one pictured here is a 4-inch (10 cm) square. The ribbon measurements are for this box; if you use a larger box, increase the ribbon measurements by 2 inches.

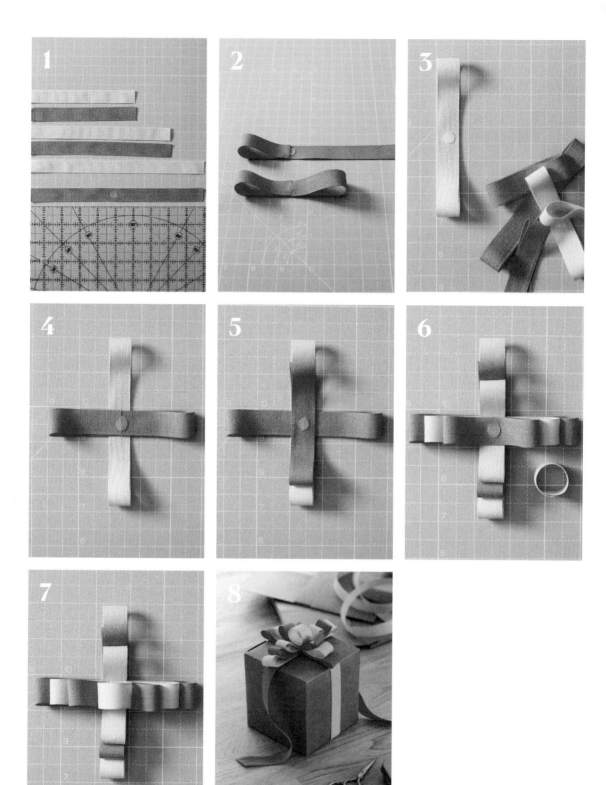

ONE Cut the two pieces of ribbon in each color into three different lengths: 6 inches (15 cm), 8 inches (20 cm), and 10 inches (25 cm).

TWO Place an adhesive dot in the center of each cut ribbon piece and press down firmly on the adhesive dot. Take one end of the ribbon and loop it to rest on top of half the adhesive dot, being careful to avoid flattening the ribbon loop. Repeat on the other side.

THREE Repeat with the remaining five ribbon pieces.

FOUR Using the largest loops first, lay one loop vertically on your work surface with the seam facing up. Place an adhesive dot at the center. Take another large loop in a different color and rest it horizontally (perpendicular) on top of the other loop.

FIVE Repeat the same steps with the two loops that are one size smaller than the first. Remember to add an adhesive dot at the center seam before stacking each ribbon loop.

SIX Continue adding ribbon pieces, alternating direction and color, until you have used all loops. The last piece can face seam down, but be sure you add an adhesive dot at the center. Cut one piece of 3-inch (7.5 cm) ribbon. Affix an adhesive dot to one end and roll the ribbon into a circle, overlapping the ends by ¼ inch (6 mm). Press down firmly.

SEVEN Place the ribbon circle on top of your loop stack.

EIGHT Wrap the box with a piece of ribbon long enough to go all around. In this case, this piece measures 17 inches (43 cm). Secure the ends on the bottom of the box with an adhesive dot, overlapping ½ inch (1.3 cm). Cut another piece of ribbon to trail off the sides of the bow. In this case, this piece measures 18 inches (46 cm). Place that ribbon on the center top of the box. Add one final adhesive dot on top of the crossed ribbon. Place the stacked ribbon loops on top. Adjust ribbon to your liking.

Adjust the colors depending on the occasion, such as all white for a wedding gift, pastels for baby gifts, or shades of red for the holidays.

Lay finished bows on the center of your table as a centerpiece.

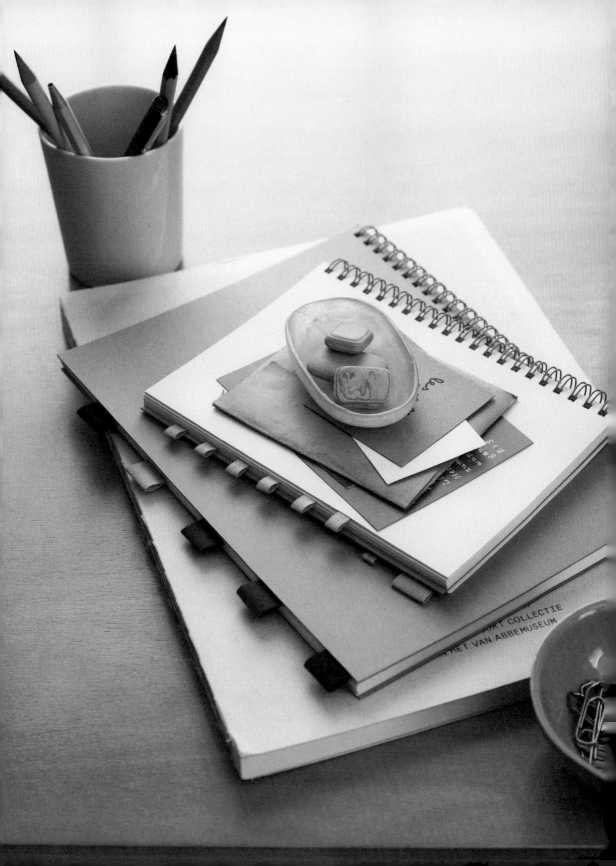

Ribbon-Tab Journal

Get organized with the help of clever color-coded ribbon tabs. This personal touch can be applied to journals, calendars, and planners.

SUPPLIES

Large spiral notebook (Ours is by MUJI, size B5, 7 × 10 inches [18 × 25 cm], 80 pages.)

Ribbon for the larger notebook: Tight weave cotton ribbon, ⅝ inch (1.5 cm) wide (pictured in the colors Wine, Brick, Navy, Ochre, and Indigo). This project calls for 10 inches (25 cm) of ribbon.

Small spiral notebook (Ours is by MUJI, size B6, 5 × 7 inches [13 × 18 cm], 80 pages.)

Ribbon for the smaller notebook: Tight weave cotton ribbon, ¼ inch (6 mm) wide (pictured in the color Pool).

Tight weave cotton ribbon, ⅝ inch (1.5 cm) wide and 2 inches (5 cm) long (pictured in the color Pool). This project calls for a total of 10½ inches (26.5 cm) of ¼-inch- (6 mm) wide ribbon and 2 inches (5 cm) of ⅝-inch- (1.5 cm) wide ribbon.

Scissors

Permanent double-sided tape, ½ inch (1.3 cm) wide (For this project, we used the brand Aniann.)

Pencil

Ruler

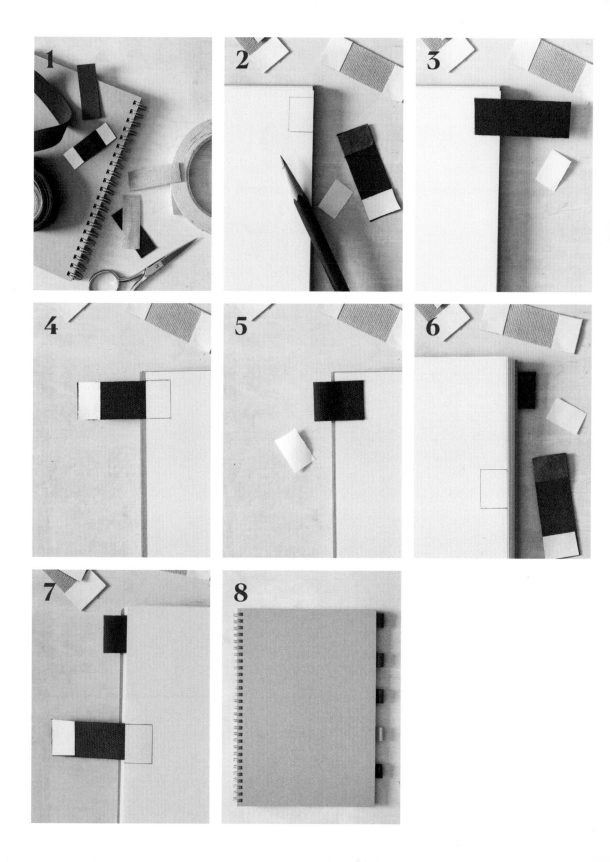

ONE For the large notebook, cut five pieces of ⅝-inch- (1.5 cm) wide ribbon measuring 2 inches (5 cm) in length.

Place a piece of double sided tape on each end of the ribbon pieces, making sure you press down well for the tape to fully adhere.

TWO Choose the page where you would like your first tab to be placed. Using a pencil, lightly mark ⅛ inch (3 mm) down from the top edge and ½ inch (1.3 cm) in from the side.

THREE Peel off the backing from tape on one end of the ribbon piece. Press ribbon onto the page within the pencil markings.

FOUR Repeat, making markings on the other side of the page.

FIVE Remove the backing of the tape on the other end of the ribbon and press the ribbon into the page just as you did with the first side. Be careful not to crease the ribbon as you create a loop.

SIX Find the page where you'd like to place your next tab. For the MUJI journal, there are 16 pages between tabs. (This is the total number of pages divided by 5 tabs.)

For the following tabs, mark 1¼ inches (3 cm) below the bottom edge of the first ribbon, again ½ inch (1.3 cm) in from the side and ⅝ inch (1.5 cm) down (the width of the ribbon).

SEVEN Repeat the steps just as before to secure each tab to the page, until all tabs are finished.

EIGHT For the smaller notebook, repeat how-to steps with one exception: Start with one ⅝-inch- (1.5 cm) wide tab at the top and then continued with seven pieces of ¼-inch- (6 mm) wide ribbon with ½ inch (1.3 cm) in between.

Use the same technique to add tabs to hanging file folders. Use the colors as an organizing principle (e.g., subject, year, priority).

Add tabs to photo albums.

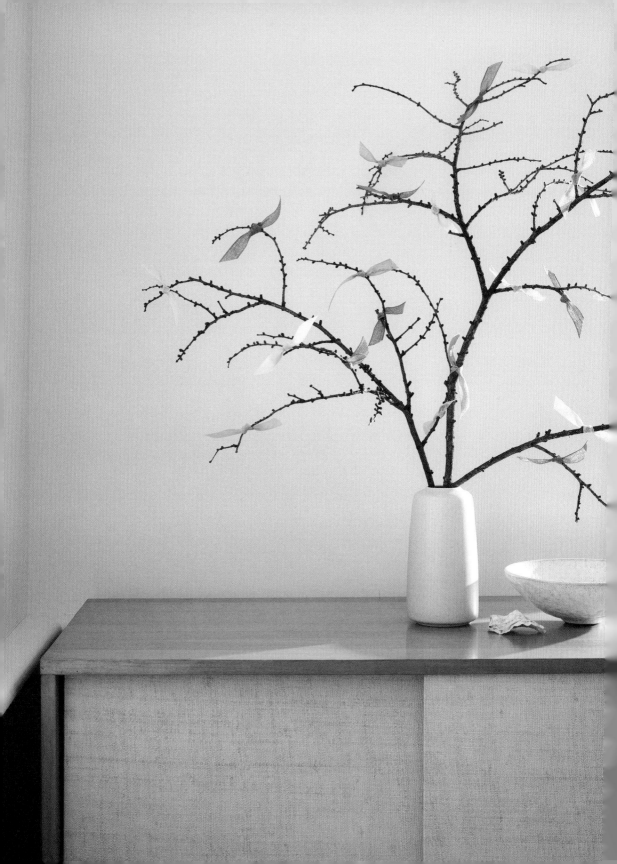

Blooming Branch

Usher in warmer weather by bringing nature indoors. Embellish a dried, foraged branch with colorful ribbon that imitates hints of budding blossoms and leaves.

SUPPLIES

Scissors

Ruler or tape measure

Loose weave ribbon, ½ inch (1.3 cm) wide (pictured in the colors Grass, Blush, and Petal). This project uses about thirty-two 5½-inch (14 cm) pieces of ribbon: twenty in shades of pink and twelve in green

Foraged branch

Vase

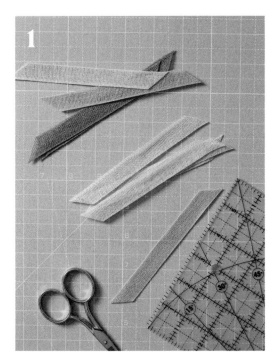

ONE Cut pieces of ribbon measuring 5½ inches (14 cm); trim both ends on a diagonal pointing the same direction. Although the amount of ribbon depends on the size of the branch, we used about thirty-two pieces for this branch (twelve green leaves and twenty pink blossoms).

TWO With the branch secure in your desired vessel, begin tying ribbon pieces with a single knot. Trim ribbon ends to clean them up a bit as needed. Start with green (your leaves), followed by pinks (your colorful blossoms).

THREE Keep tying ribbons—taking a step back to check for gaps and proper spacing—until the desired look is achieved.

Adjust the colors of the ribbons depending on the seasons.

Tie ribbons around the ends of floral wire and tuck into a floral bouquet.

Tie ribbons around Christmas tree branches.

Tie ribbons around the handle of an Easter or gift basket.

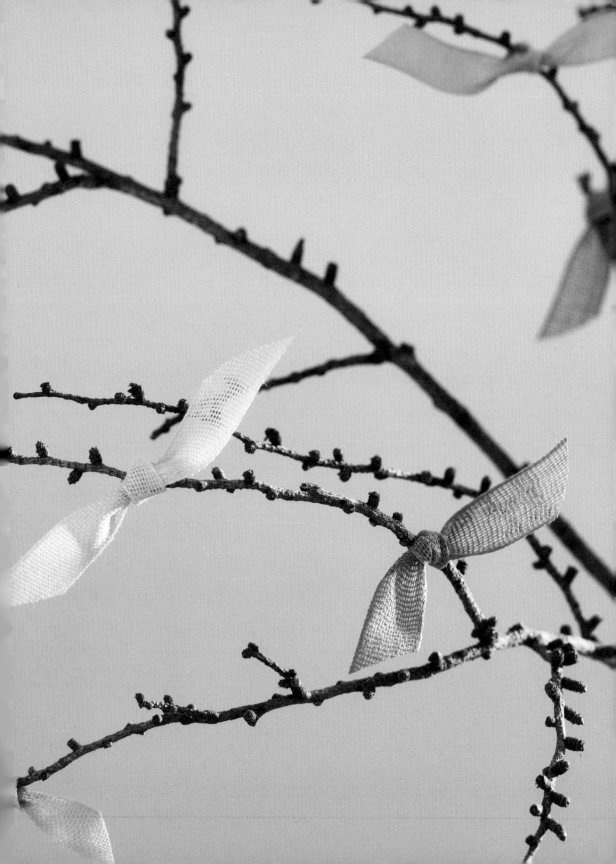

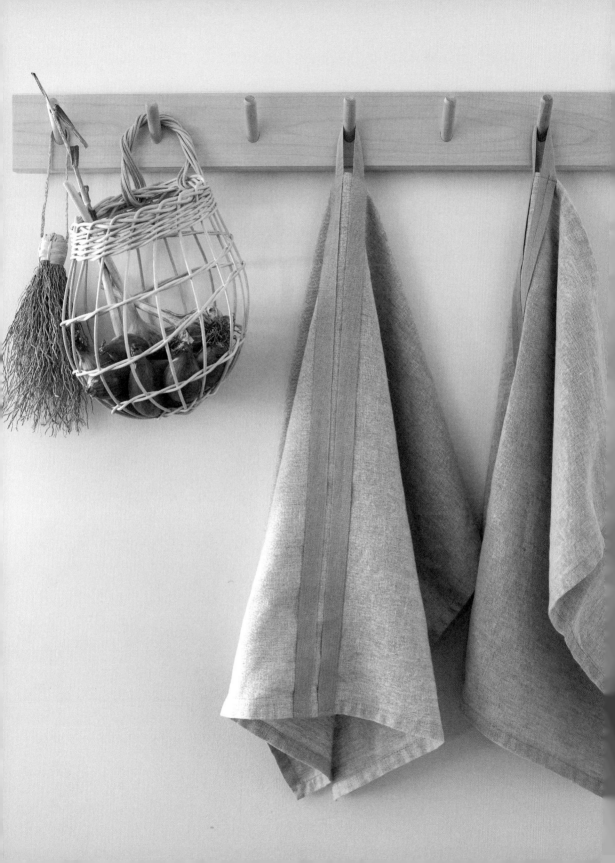

Ribbon-Trim Tea Towel

Give a simple linen tea towel new life with a pop of colorful ribbon. Add a loop for easy hanging (and added prettiness). Gift them as a set or keep them for use in your own kitchen.

SUPPLIES

Quilting ruler

Linen tea towel (Ours measures 27 × 19½ inches [69 × 49.5 cm].)

Fabric marker

Tight weave cotton ribbon, ⅝ inch (1.5 cm) wide (pictured in the colors Ice and Ochre). This project calls for 50 inches (127 cm) of each color of ribbon.

Straight sewing pins

Sewing needle and thread

Scissors

Note: To prevent shrinkage, prewash both towel and ribbon. Prewash the ribbon by soaking it in hot water for an hour or so, then hanging until almost dry and ironing well. (It's easier to iron while still slightly damp.) Remember to test for color fastness, as explained in the Ribbon Basics section (page 39).

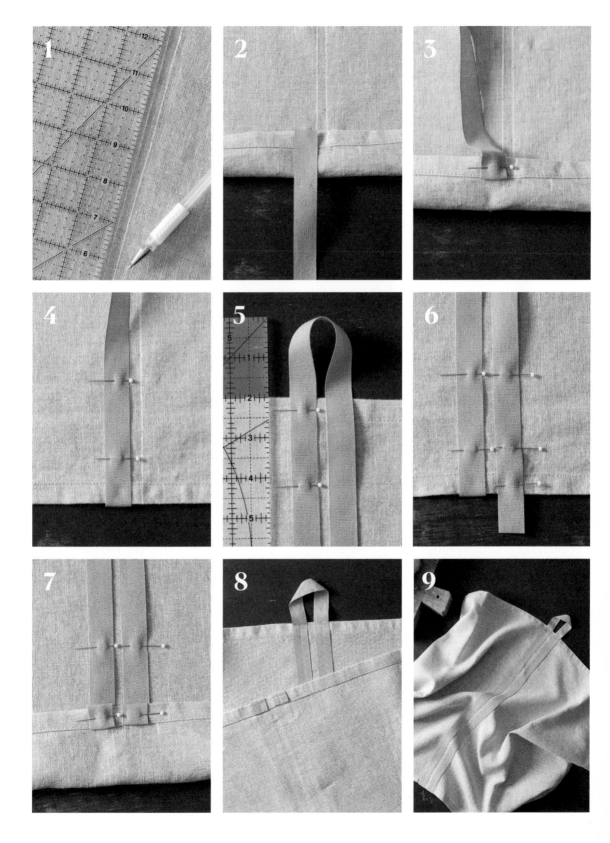

ONE Measure the width of your towel and use a fabric marker to mark the center at both the top and bottom of the towel. For this project, we stitched our ribbon onto the towel down the center on its horizontal side. You could stitch on the vertical side for a different look.

TWO From the center mark, measure ⅛ inch (3 mm) on the left and the right side and mark again. From those points, draw two long lines down the tea towel to serve as your guide. On the underside of the towel, line up the ribbon with the edge of the towel.

THREE At the hemline of the towel—in our case, that's at ½ inch (1.3 cm)—fold the ribbon back over itself and pin in place. Fold the ribbon over to the front side of the towel.

FOUR Pin ribbon along your guideline all the way to the top edge of the towel. Once you reach the top, extend the ribbon 2 inches (5 cm) beyond the top edge.

FIVE Bring the ribbon back down toward the towel, creating a loop.

SIX Continue pinning along your guideline.

SEVEN When you reach the bottom edge, turn the underside of the towel upward. Fold the end of your ribbon ½ inch (1.3 cm) under twice and pin, again lined up with the hemline.

EIGHT Stitch all the way down the center of each ribbon, removing the pins as you go. Then sew across the base of the ribbon loop, ⅛ inch (3 mm) from the top edge for reinforcement.

NINE Repeat at the other end of the tea towel across the ribbon, ⅛ inch (3 mm) from the bottom edge.

TIP If your tea towel is a different size, you will need ribbon that measures double the height of your towel, plus 2 inches (5 cm) to fold under the ends, plus 4 inches (10 cm) for the loop.

You can also use the same technique (without the loop accent) on a decorative pillow.

Or, try sewing one (or a few) ribbons along the edge of a curtain.

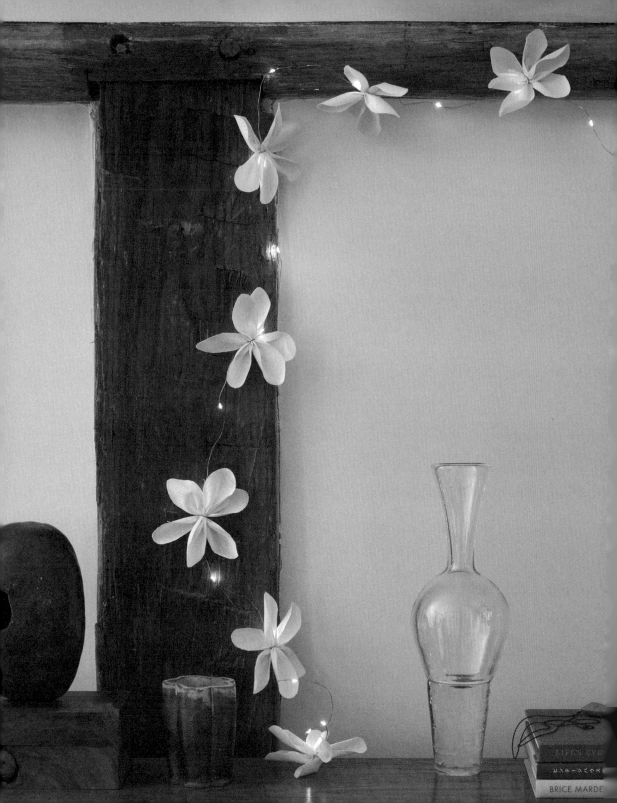

Flowering Garland

Ribbon is transformed into a flowering garland or decor for your next fete! Store and save for celebrations to come.

SUPPLIES

Ribbon scissors

Tight weave cotton ribbon, 1½ inches (4 cm) wide (pictured in the color Natural). This project calls for 4½ yards (4.2 m) of ribbon.

Pencil

Card stock

Disappearing-ink fabric marker

Extra-strong sewing thread or embroidery floss in matching color

28-gauge copper wire

Craft scissors or wire cutters

Battery-operated fairy-light strand, 7 inches (18.3 cm) long

Note: The ribbon edges will fray naturally, resembling real flowers. If you prefer that the edges stay crisp, dab them in clear nail polish or watered-down white glue (as explained in the Ribbon Basics section on page 39).

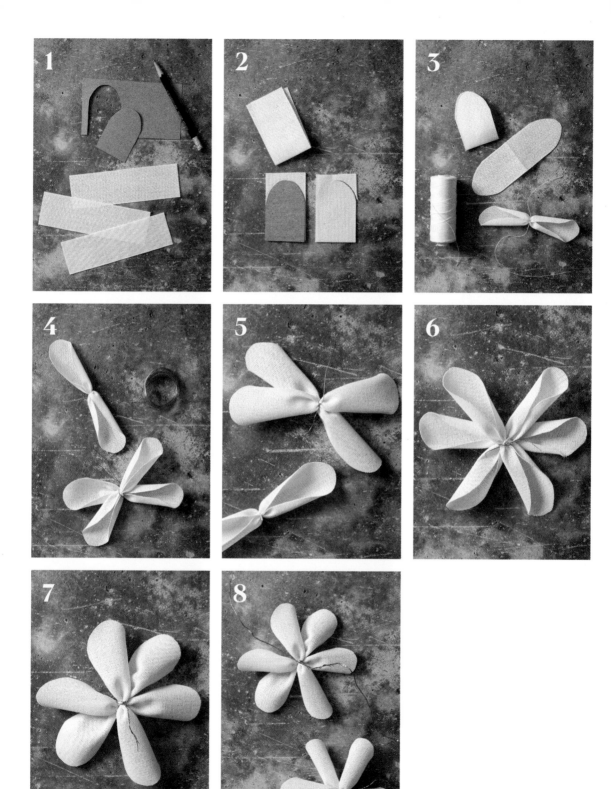

ONE Cut three pieces of ribbon measuring 5 inches (13 cm) in length. Draw a petal shape and trace it onto cardstock. Cut out. Fold each ribbon piece in half.

TWO Line up the base of the petal template with the folded crease of ribbon. Trace using a disappearing-ink fabric marker. If using a pencil, ensure you cut inside the trace lines, so they are not visible on the finished flower. Cut out the petal through both layers of ribbon.

THREE Repeat with the other two pieces. Open petals. Lay one petal on top of a strong thread (such as a buttonhole thread) at the center crease line. Tie a loose knot at the center. As you pull tightly, attempt to have the petal creases fold in evenly. It doesn't need to be precise, but it is helpful if they fold in the same direction on both sides and do not twist. Add a second knot to secure and snip ends.

FOUR Repeat with the other two pieces. Lay one petal horizontal onto your work surface; lay a second piece on top at a slight diagonal. Cut a 6-inch (15 cm) length of copper wire. (You can use old craft scissors to do this, spare your precious ribbon scissors!) Lay the wire centered on top of the petal stack. Wrap the wire around the center of the petal stack.

FIVE Twist the wire at the bottom of the flower.

SIX Bring the wire around and back up to the top through the opposite petals to make sure the shape is secure and the petals are connected. Lay a third petal on top of the other two (resting it between the two wire ends) to create a flower shape.

SEVEN Wrap wire around the center of the petal stack. Bring it back to the bottom of the flower and twist the wire firmly until you reach the end. In doing so, you will tighten the petals of your ribbon flower. Turn the flower over. Straighten petals as needed and remove any residue from the disappearing-ink fabric marker. Make additional flowers. For this 7-inch (18.3 cm) garland of lights, we made ten flowers.

EIGHT Using the twisted wire length, connect each flower to the garland of lights by twisting lightly. Once you find the desired spacing and arrangement of your flowers, tighten the wires.

Cut the ends of the flowers into points, instead of rounded edges, and swap in red ribbon for an instant poinsettia holiday garland.

Use the same technique to make flowers to pin onto a wreath form.

Wire flowers to a hairpin or use floral wire to make stems.

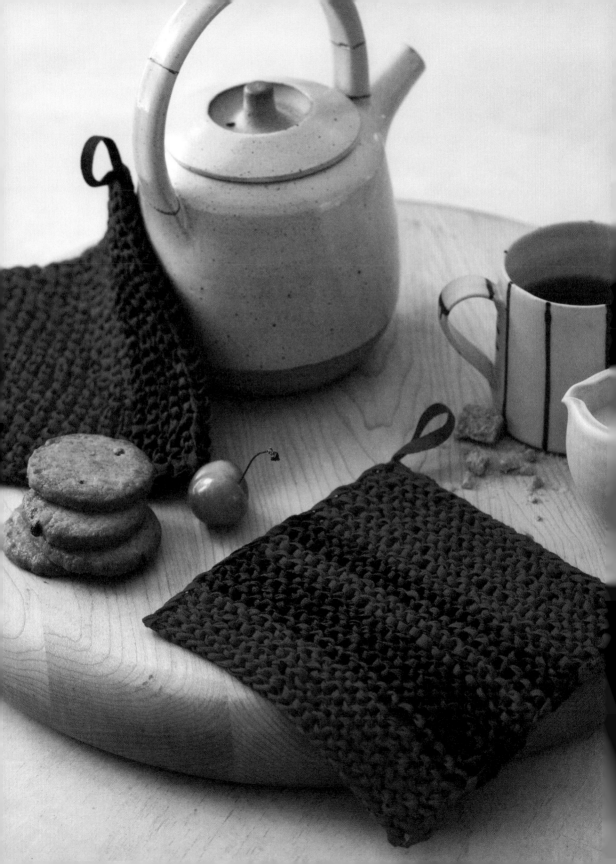

Garter Stitch Potholder

Knit—then use, gift, or admire—sturdy potholders using ribbon. Yes, you can knit with ribbon!

SUPPLIES

Tight weave cotton ribbon, ¼ inch (6 mm) wide (pictured in the colors Iron and Red). This project calls for around 35 yards (32 m) of ribbon.

Size US 10 (6 mm) knitting needles

Tapestry needle

Gauge:
15 stitches and 30 rows = 4 inches (10 cm) square in garter stitch. Follow the 4-inch (10 cm) gauge with the tension of your knit to achieve the correct final measurement.

The finished project dimensions are 6 inches (15 cm) square.

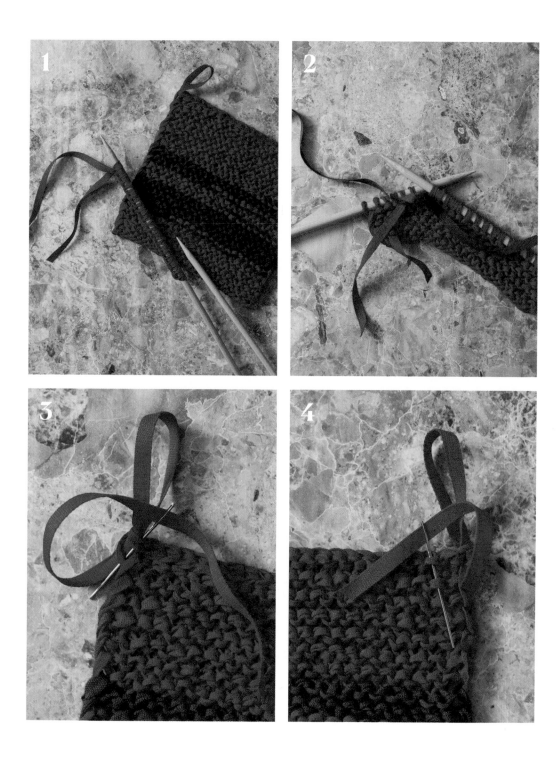

ONE Cast on 24 stitches using a basic long-tail cast-on.

Row 1: Slip 1 purlwise with ribbon in front, then knit to the end of the row. Repeat Row 1 until desired color change.

TWO Slip 1 purlwise with yarn in front, knit 8 stitches in garter stitch with first color. Cut ribbon. Leaving a 3-inch (7.5 cm) tail, change to a new color and continue until the end of the row.

Continue knitting with the new color until desired color change, or until your piece measures 6 inches (15 cm) high. Because each potholder and ribbon are different, each stripe will be different. You will knit the number of stitches to achieve the width of stripe that you want, as shown in photos 1 and 2. With the right side facing you, bind off your stitches until you have 1 stitch left. Pull the ribbon so that stitch creates a 1½-inch (4 cm) high loop. Cut the ribbon leaving a 5-inch (13 cm) tail.

THREE Thread the end of the ribbon onto a tapestry needle. Stitch through the prior stitch and back out through the last stitch, so that the loop fastens.

FOUR Weave in the ends, following the stitches of the pattern. Cut the ribbon end. Weave in remaining ends and gently wet block as desired.

NOTE Knitting with ribbon is different from yarn, due to the flat nature of the ribbon (versus the round nature of yarn). The result is a less-even knit structure, though that is what gives this project character. You may choose to keep the yarn flat, rather than twist while knitting. That might mean a slower worked knit. It might also make for a less precise gauge, but if you knit it to become a square, it will look (and work) just right.

CARE INSTRUCTIONS Hand wash and lay out to dry on a flat surface.

Stitch two pieces together on three sides; add a ribbon as a strap and it becomes a little bag.

Stitch two larger pieces together and create a decorative pillowcase.

Use as trivets and/or potholders.

Make a smaller section and use it as a "rug" in a dollhouse.

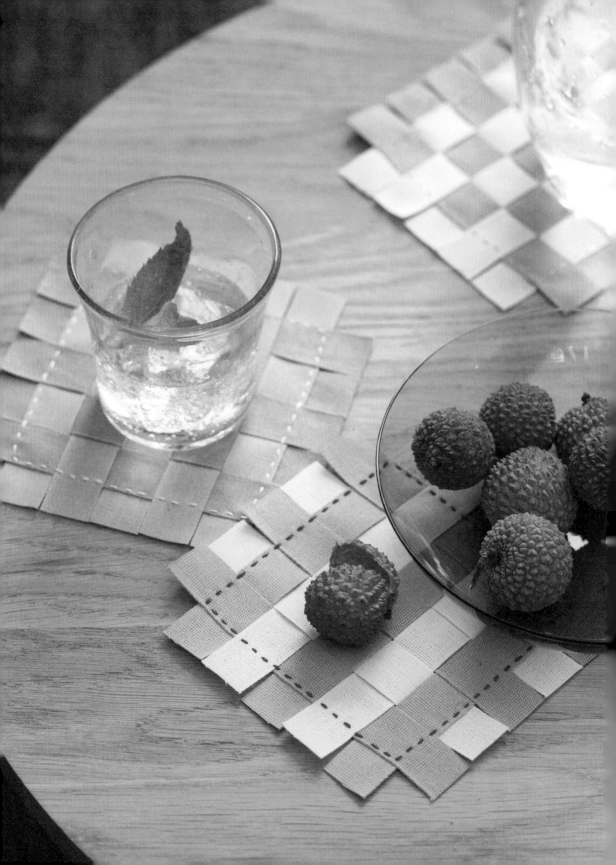

Woven Coaster

Woven ribbon makes a colorful cushion for your cocktail or coffee. Make multiples—this project makes for a great assembly line craft.

SUPPLIES

Scissors

Tight weave cotton ribbon, ⅝ inch wide (pictured in the colors Natural, Ice, and Chartreuse). This project calls for about 28 inches (71 cm) of ribbon in each color.

Painter's tape

Embroidery floss

Sewing needle

Quilter's ruler

Rotary cutter

Clear nail polish

Note: The instructions below are for a checkered pattern. You can make any pattern you'd like by playing around with the order of horizontal and vertical ribbon colors.

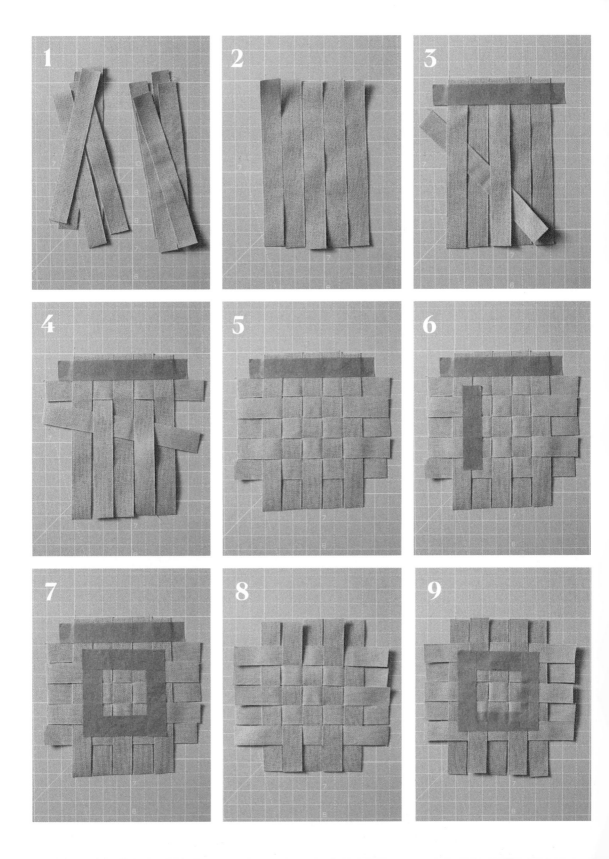

ONE Cut five pieces of ribbon measuring 5½ inches (14 cm) from two of the colors—ten pieces total. Or if you are making a stripe pattern, cut six pieces of one color, and four of the other.

TWO Lay five of the pieces in the same color close to one another (alternate colors for a stripe pattern). Tip: Use a ruled cutting mat to help keep your ribbon nice and straight.

THREE Create a "weft" (the crosswise threads on a loom) by using a piece of painter's tape to adhere the tops of the ribbon to your work surface.

Begin weaving a piece of ribbon in an alternate color horizontally into the weft.

Shimmy that piece all the way up to meet and be parallel with the tape. Leave the same amount of excess length on both sides. (You will trim this later.)

FOUR Repeat by weaving the next piece of ribbon (if you are making a stripe pattern, use your alternate color) to meet the first, but instead of weaving under the first vertical ribbon, go over it (weave under the second).

FIVE Continue in the same fashion with the remaining three pieces (alternating colors if you are making a stripe pattern).

SIX Once finished, apply a piece of painter's tape ⅜ inch (1 cm) below the top taped edge and along the side edge, down to ⅜ (1 cm) up from the bottom edge to keep ribbon pieces from shifting.

SEVEN Continue taping all around, ⅜ inch (1 cm) from the edges, straightening the ribbon if needed.

EIGHT Remove the tape from the top edge (the piece you used to create your weft). Turn over.

NINE Apply tape in the same way as you did on the other side.

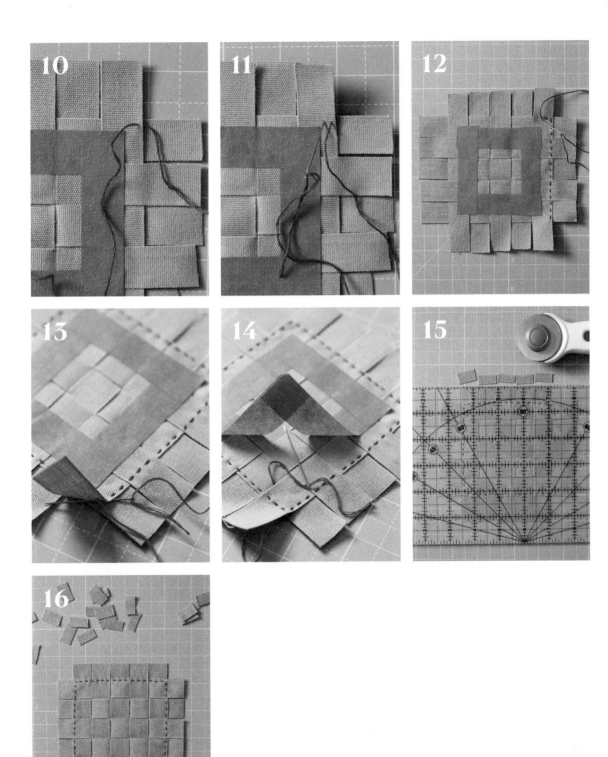

TEN Cut a 22-inch (56 cm) piece of embroidery floss and pull three strands of the floss apart from the rest. Thread one section of floss onto your sewing needle and make a knot about 1 inch (2.5 cm) from the other end. Starting on one corner of your coaster, insert the needle from between the warp and weft / vertical and horizontal piece, about ⅛ inch (3 mm) from both edges.

ELEVEN Pull the thread so the knot and end hide between the two layers. Pull the needle/thread up toward you. Reinsert the needle back down with a small stitch, about ⅛ inch (3 mm) in length, going through both layers and having the needle come out on the other side. Pull the thread to stitch taught.

TWELVE Continue using a running stitch all the way around, making sure the stitches are even in spacing and placement on both front and back.

THIRTEEN When you get to the last corner, insert the needle between the last two layers of the warp/weft. Stitch the end of the thread behind the first stitch, loop around, and insert the needle again to create a knot. Repeat to make sure it is fastened.

FOURTEEN Push the needle between the layers, outward, and snip. This ensures the floss end is hidden between layers. Remove painter's tape from both sides.

FIFTEEN Using a quilting ruler and a rotary cutter, trim the ends of all four sides to ⅝ inch (1.5 cm) beyond the edge of your woven square. Press firmly on the ruler as you cut.

SIXTEEN To prevent fraying, dab each ribbon end with a small amount of clear nail polish. Hand wash, dry flat, and iron (hot setting) when needed.

NOTE We love the idea of a placemat-size project, but anything larger than the coaster size won't hold its shape as well using this technique.

Depending on the order of the colors, you can create different patterns.

Play with using more than just two colors, random repeats, or keep them all solid.

Assign a color to each guest to avoid confusing glasses. Or, you can shift the "drink vibe" from a refreshing lemon water to an elegant cocktail.

Use the coaster under a vase or candle holder for a more permanent display in your home.

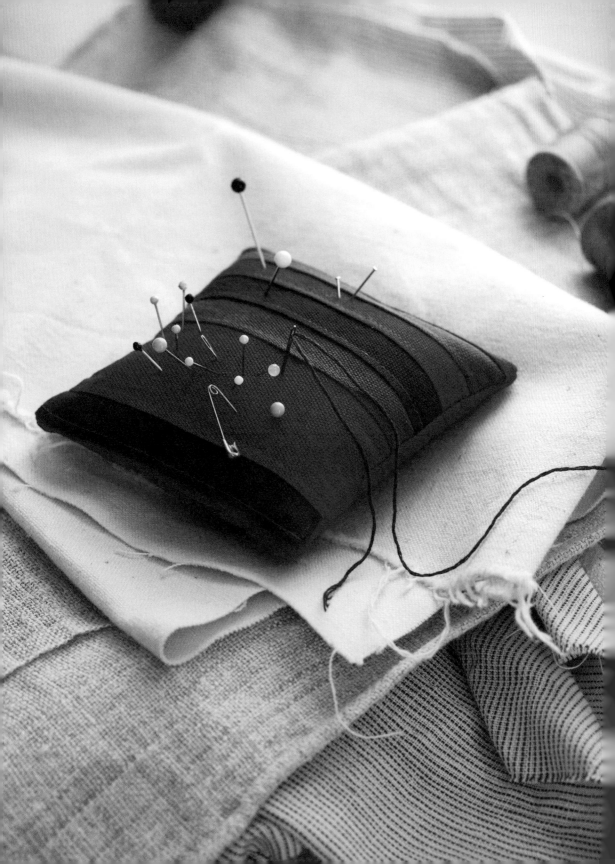

Heirloom Pincushion

Layer and sew together ribbon in various widths and colors to create a pincushion. This is a great project for special ribbon you've been saving, and the result is certainly worth passing on to the next generation.

SUPPLIES

Tight weave cotton ribbon, ⅝ inch (1.5 cm) wide and 1½ inches (4 cm) wide (pictured in the colors Red, Wine, and Brick). This project calls for 2 yards (1.8 m) of ⅝-inch- (1.5 cm) wide ribbon and 10 inches (25 cm) of 1½-inch- (4 cm) wide ribbon.

Wash away wonder tape

Basic sewing supplies (scissors, sewing thread, pins, needles, iron)

Quilting ruler

Rotary cutter

Stuffing material (Wool is pictured here. Tip: Ground walnut shells are a great alternative for their weight, plus they sharpen pins!)

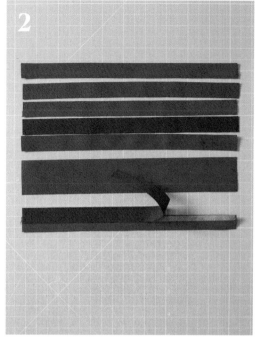

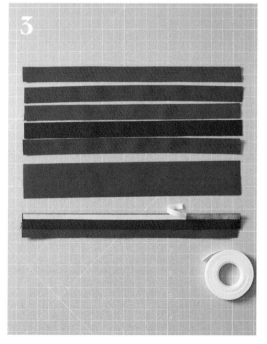

ONE Cut seven pieces of 10-inch (25 cm) lengths of ⅝-inch- (1.5 cm) wide ribbon. Cut one piece of 10-inch (25 cm) length of 1½-inch- (4 cm) wide ribbon. Adhere wonder tape across the top edge of the first piece of ribbon.

TWO Peel off protective paper on tape. Take the second piece of ribbon and line up the bottom edge of the ribbon with the bottom edge of the tape, overlapping the ribbon by ¼ inch (6 mm).

THREE Making sure everything is straight, press down firmly to adhere both pieces of ribbon together. Place wonder tape on the second ribbon piece, again lining up with the top edge. Peel off the protective paper on the tape. Press firmly.

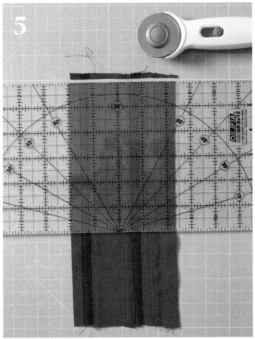

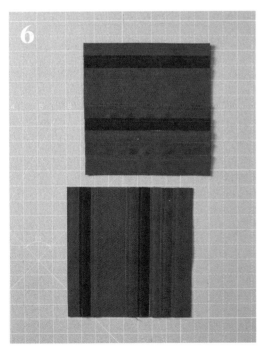

FOUR Follow these steps until all your ribbon pieces have been layered and adhered to one another. Top stitch all the ribbons with a ¹⁄₁₆-inch (1.5 mm) seam, creating one large piece of connected ribbon pieces.

FIVE Using a quilting ruler and rotary cutter, trim the top and bottom edges of your piece so they are straight.

SIX Measure the width of your piece and trim to create two equal-size square pieces. Lay squares flat and rotate one square so that the stripes of ribbon go opposite ways. When you go to connect the squares together, this makes sewing a bit easier (as you do not need to line up the stripes or navigate around multiple seams for each stripe).

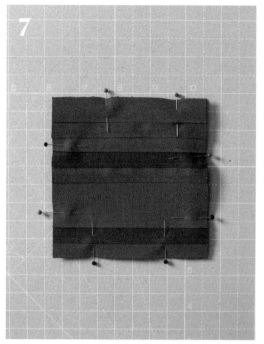

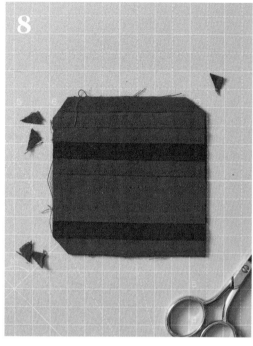

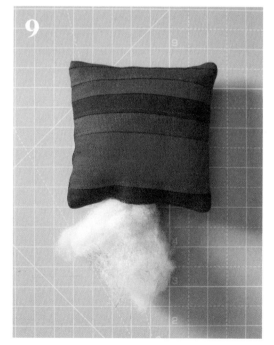

SEVEN Pin together with the right sides facing each other.

EIGHT Stitch all around the square with a ⅜-inch (1 cm) seam, leaving a 3- to 4-inch (7½ to 10 cm) opening to add stuffing. Trim corners.

NINE Turn your cushion right side out, making sure you pop the corners outward. (Tip: A chopstick can help with this!) Iron pincushion on a cotton setting. Stuff pincushion, ensuring that the stuffing fills each corner well.

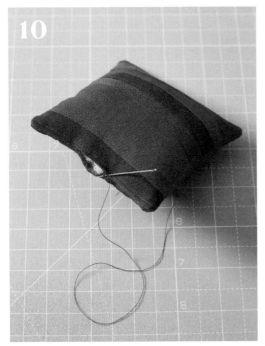

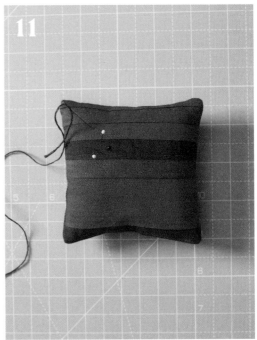

TEN Blind stitch the opening closed to complete.

ELEVEN Use your finished pin cushion to store the supplies used to make it!

Stuff your cushion with lavender or cedar shavings for a sachet.

Make several in various colors so each kind of pin in your sewing supplies arsenal gets their own pillow.

It is not suitable to make large pieces, since this ribbon will start to warp. (I wouldn't go beyond a 12-inch [30.5 cm] square) or make several pieces and, instead of sewing them into a pillow, stitch the sides to each other to create a patchwork type fabric you can then make into a pillow.

Stitch a few ribbons together, then use that piece and applique it onto a canvas bag or zip pouch.

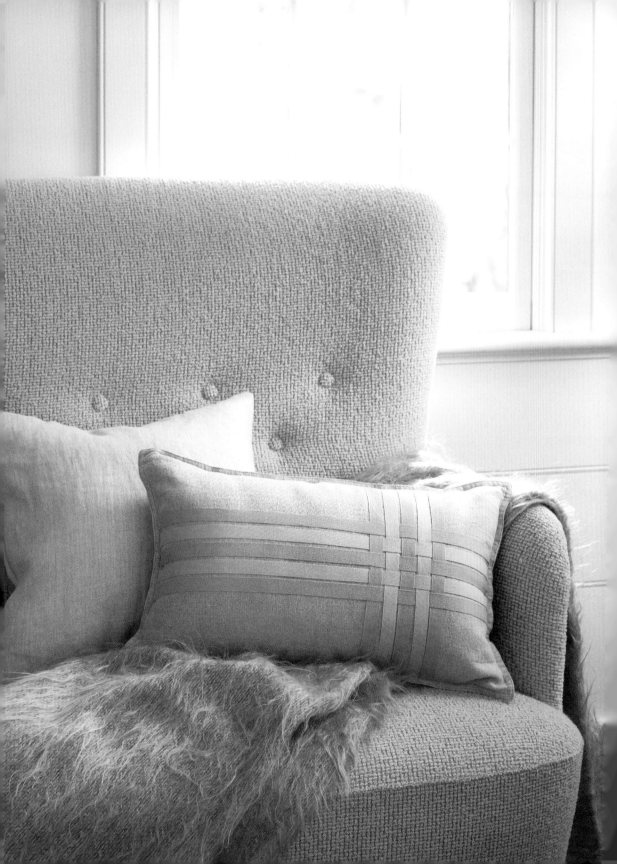

Pretty Pillow

Transform a simple pillow into a statement pillow with a woven ribbon embellishment. Play with different colors and woven patterns once you've mastered the technique.

Cardboard

Simple linen pillow. The pillow pictured is 12 × 19½ inches (30.5 × 49.5 cm). If your pillow is a different dimension, see the tip below to calculate the amount of ribbon needed.

Fabric marker

Clear quilting ruler

Scissors

Tight weave cotton ribbon, ⅝ inch (1.5 cm) wide (pictured in the colors Chartreuse and Tan). This project calls for about 3 yards (2.7 m) of Chartreuse and 2 yards (1.8 m) of Tan.

Pins

Sewing needle and thread (The thread color should match the pillow color. Here we've used a contrasting thread to better illustrate stitching how-to.)

Note: If your pillow size is different than ours, measure one vertical and one horizontal line on your desired grid, adding 1 inch (2.5 cm) to each measurement. Add those up and multiply them by the number of lines for your desired grid to figure out the total amount of ribbon needed.

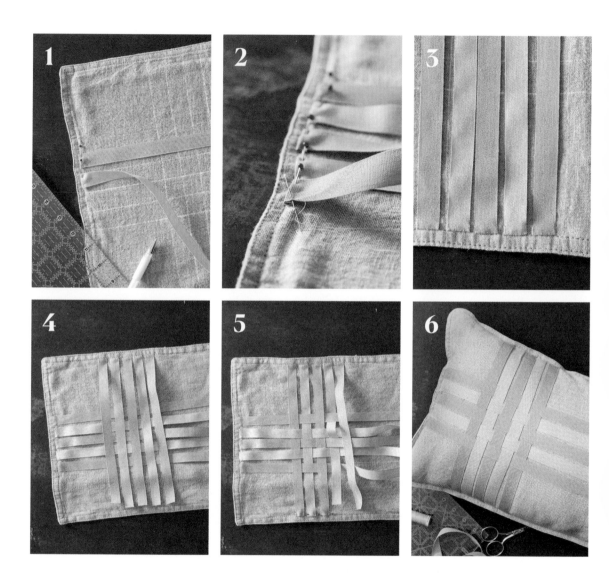

ONE Slip a piece of cardboard inside the pillowcase while you work; this is to ensure you don't stitch through both sides when sewing the ribbon to the pillow. Using a fabric marker, make a grid on the front of your pillow. The pillow pictured is 12 × 19.5 inches (30.5 × 49.5 cm). Mark the first line 4 inches (10 cm) from the top edge both horizontally and vertically, followed by five additional lines spaced 7/8 inch (2.2 cm) apart. Measure one vertical and one horizontal line on your grid, adding 1 inch (2.5 cm) to each measurement before cutting five pieces of ribbon per length in desired colors.

Fold each piece of ribbon ¼ inch (6 mm), and then again ¼ inch (6 mm). Adhere a horizontal ribbon piece to the pillow with pins. Line up the top of the ribbon with each marker line.

TWO Repeat with pinning the other four ribbons in place on the same side, ensuring you catch the folded edge of each ribbon end. Alternate colors to create the pattern pictured.

THREE Stitch ribbon onto pillow with matching color thread, making sure you catch the folded edge.

FOUR Repeat pinning and sewing ends of vertical ribbons.

FIVE Weave ribbons in an over-under pattern as pictured. Fold the ends of the ribbon lengths under twice by ¼ inch (6 mm) as before and pin in place.

SIX Sew all the ribbon ends in place until the grid is complete. Add additional stitches to grid corners (and every inch or so along ribbons) as needed.

Play with different widths of ribbon, and/or dimensions and proportions of your pillow base. Experiment with the placement of your "weaving" and you'll come up with a whole fleet of pillows for your sofa. Shift the ribbon colors according to your decor.

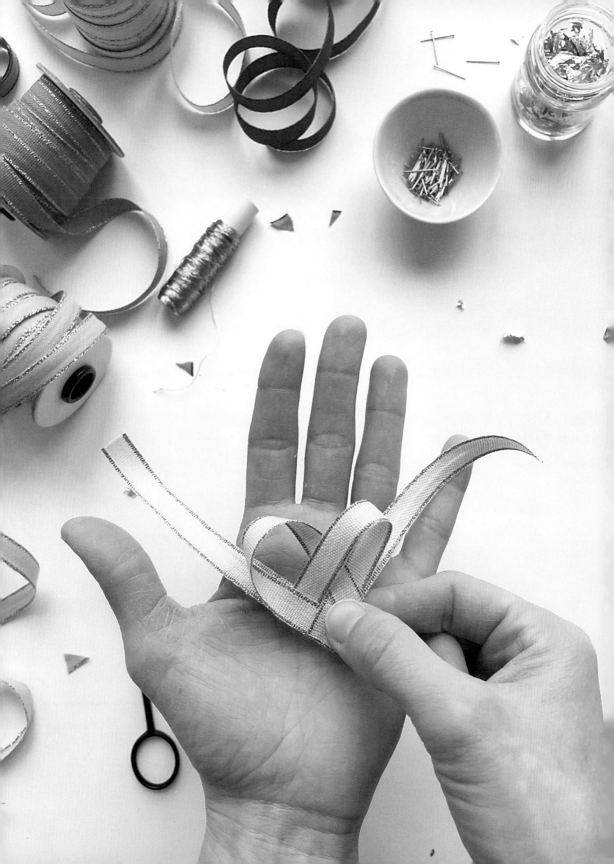

RIBBON ORNAMENTS FOR EVERY SEASON

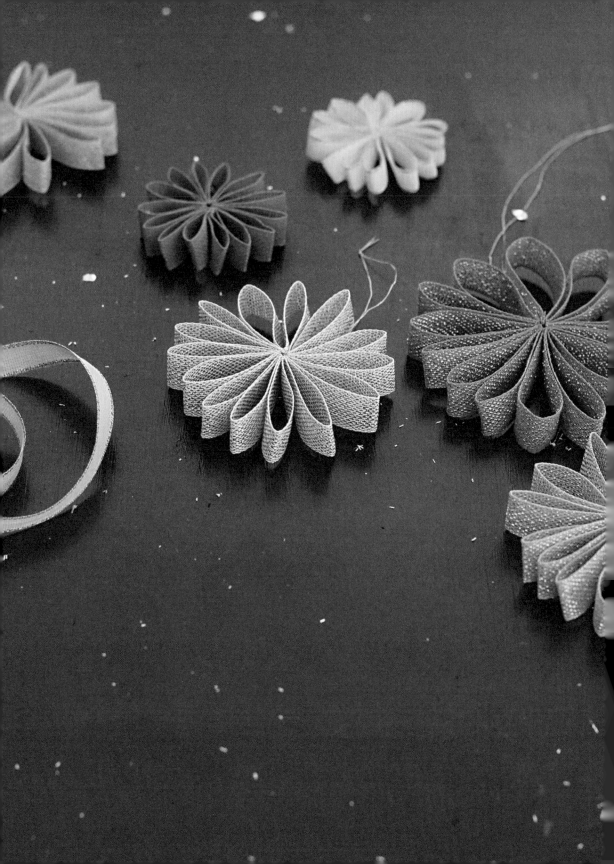

Starry Night Ribbon Ornaments

Usher in the holidays by making glittering star ornaments from metallic ribbons. The flecks of gold and silver woven into the ribbon add a gorgeous luster to each star. Make multiple ornaments to hang on your tree, use as gift toppers, or give as gifts themselves. (They are that special!)

SUPPLIES

Scissors

Metallic ribbon

Fray check or watered-down glue

Sewing needle and thread

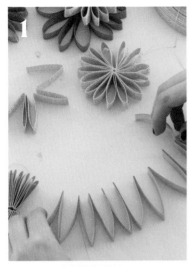

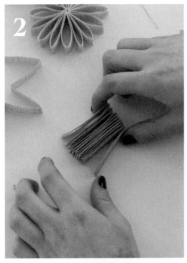

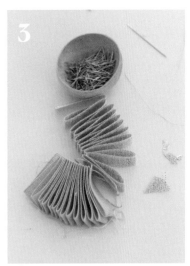

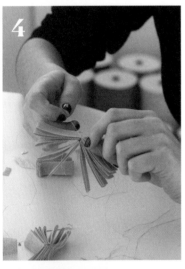

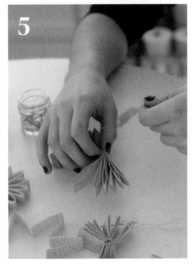

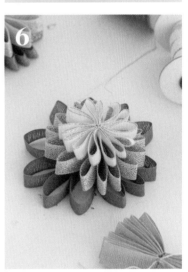

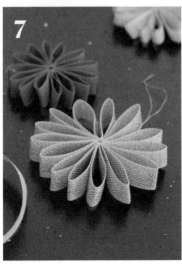

ONE Cut a piece of metallic ribbon measuring 45 inches (114 cm). Add fray check or watered-down white glue to each end in order to prevent fraying. Cut a piece of strong thread measuring 8 inches (20 cm) long, thread it through a needle, and set aside. Measure 1½ inches (4 cm) from the end of the metallic ribbon and begin folding it back and forth on itself—accordion style—until you have fourteen loops.

TWO You'll want to make sure they are the same length each time you fold by holding the stack of loops together in one hand.

THREE Starting on one corner of the ribbon stack, close to the edge or fold, insert the threaded needle through two layers of ribbon and secure with a backstitch, leaving a 3-inch (7.5 cm) tail. Gently push the needle through the top of each loop until the full stack is connected. Leave the thread untied. Thread needle with another length of 8-inch (20 cm) thread and repeat steps 3 and 4 on the other corner.

FOUR Once all the way through the stack, tie the ends of one set of the threads together, pulling the loops tight to knot.

FIVE Do the same thing on the other side: Tie the ends of the second set of threads together and form a knot.

SIX Form the ribbon loops into a circle, arranging them evenly by pinching in the center and top of each loop.

SEVEN Stitch a length of gold thread through the top of one loop and knot to hang.

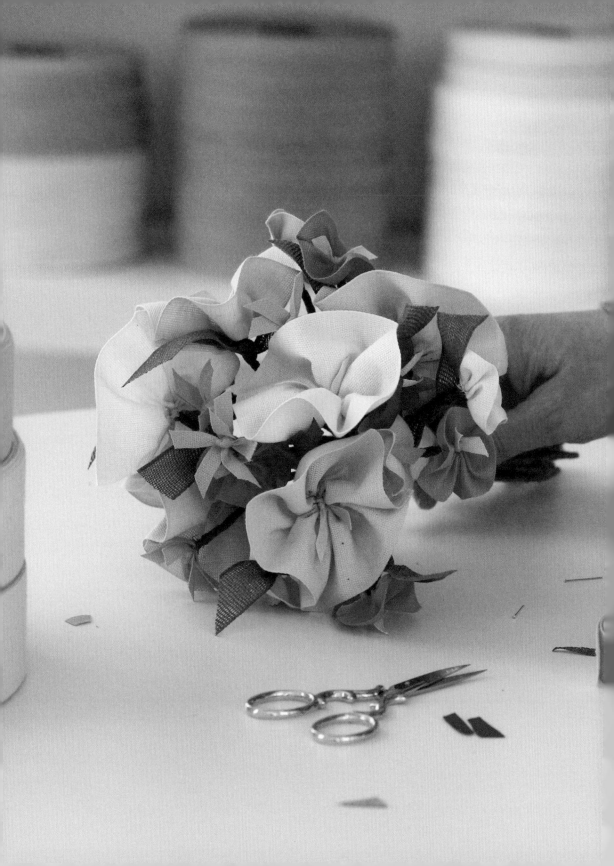

Flower Bouquet

These ribbon flowers can be made in an assembly line. Make one bloom for a bud vase or to slip atop a gift, or create the whole bouquet in an array of shapes and sizes. The best part? These blossoms don't need water.

SUPPLIES

Assorted ribbons:
For the large blooms, use tight weave cotton ribbon, 1½ inches (4 cm) wide.
For the smaller flowers, use tight weave cotton ribbon, ⅝ inch (1.5 cm) wide.
For the stamen of the flower, use tight weave cotton ribbon, ¼ inch (6 mm) wide.

Loose weave cotton ribbon in green

Scissors

Floral wire (We used 24-gauge cloth stem wire.)

Sewing needle and thread

Fray check or watered-down glue (optional)

Craft glue

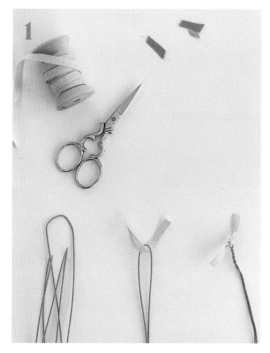

ONE To create the stamen of the flower, cut a piece of the ¼-wide (6 mm) ribbon measuring 2½ inches (6.5 cm). Fold one piece of floral wire in half. Slide the ribbon through the bent floral wire and twist the wire to encase the ribbon. Tie off with a knot.

TWO Cut a piece of the 1½-inch- (4 cm) wide ribbon measuring 10 inches (25 cm). (If making a smaller flower, use the ⅝-inch- (1.5 cm) wide ribbon in pieces measuring ½ inch.) Using strong sewing thread or two threads doubled-up, sew a running stitch for about 4 inches (10 cm) (For the smaller flower, stitch all the way to the end with a running stitch.) Be sure to secure the first stitch with a few backstitches.

THREE Gently pull the thread and the ribbon will begin to gather to create a bunched, or petal-like, shape. Secure gathers with a few backstitches.

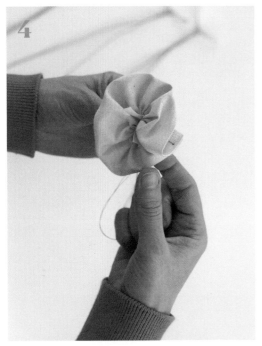

FOUR Continue stitching and gathering until you've gone all the way around. Secure with a few backstitches.

FIVE Insert the stem into the center of the flower. To close the flower, match the ends of ribbon and stitch together with a running stitch.

SIX To adhere the stem to the flower, stitch stem and flower together ensuring you've gone through the layers a few times. Trim any excess ribbon at seam. If you'd like, dab a bit of fray check or watered-down glue on the raw edges of the ribbon to prevent fraying.

SEVEN Cut a 15-inch (38 cm) piece of loose weave green ribbon. (Cut on an angle to ensure a nice seam!) At the very top of the stem, as close to the petals as possible, begin tightly wrapping the ribbon around the wire downward, overlapping slightly each time. Add a dab of glue at the bottom and hold in place for a moment to adhere.

EIGHT To create ribbon "leaves," cut 6-inch (15 cm) pieces of loose weave ribbon and tie around the stem where desired. Cut ends at an angle.

NINE Slip one atop a gift or recreate the whole bouquet. Enjoy!

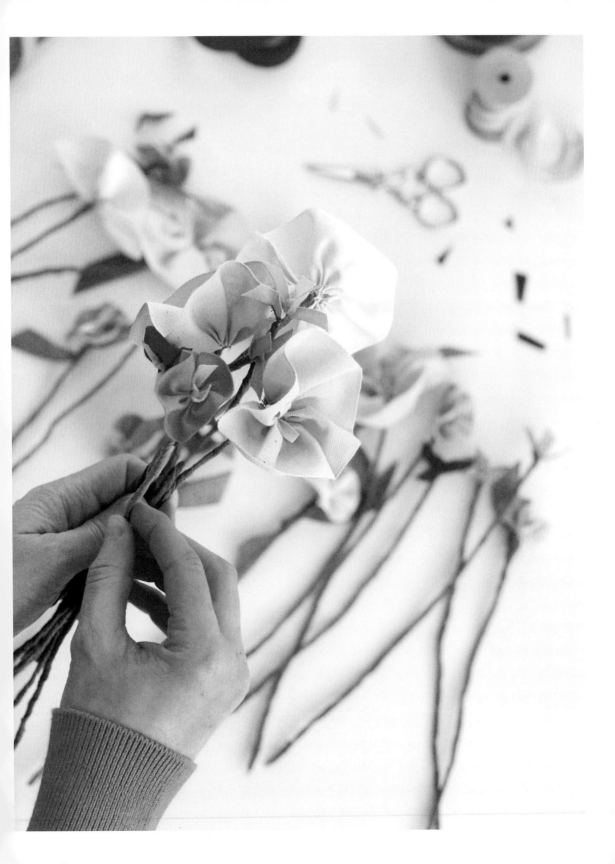

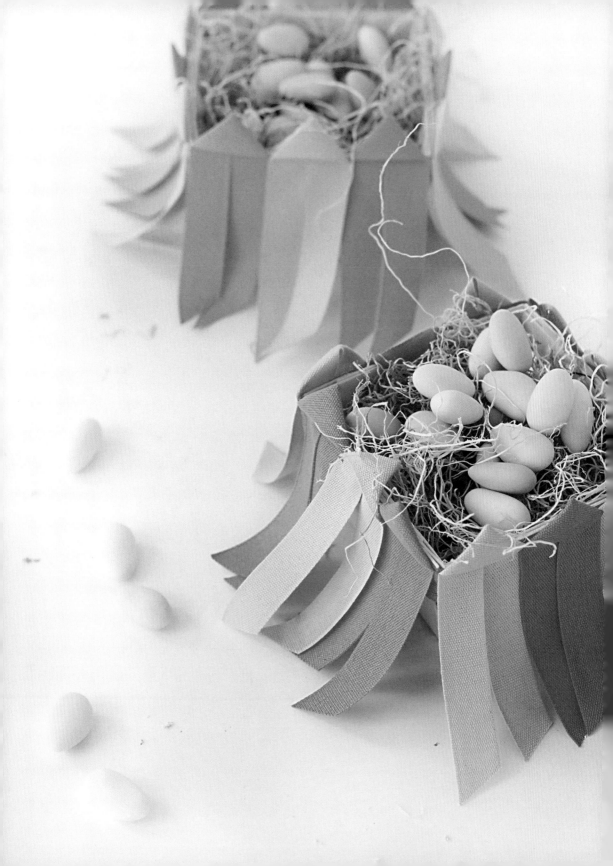

Spring
Nests

It's officially spring when we're dreaming of warmer weather and displaying our brightest colored ribbons. Nature stirs, and spring holidays are right around the corner. Create beautiful DIY nests using colorful cotton ribbons, chip wood berry baskets, and a few simple notions.

SUPPLIES

Measuring tape

Chipwood berry baskets

Scissors

Tight weave cotton ribbon, ⅝ inch (1.5 cm) wide

Straight pins

Drittofilo or ⅜-inch- (10 mm) wide ribbon

Sewing needle and thread

Craft glue

Wood excelsior, for filling the nest

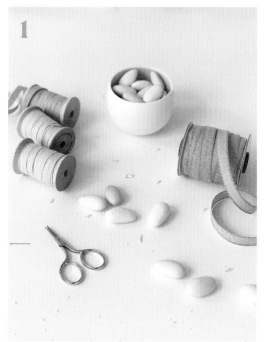

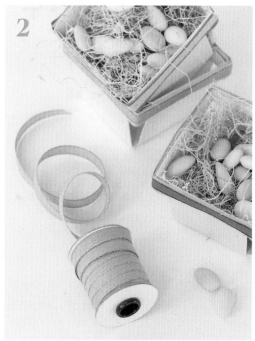

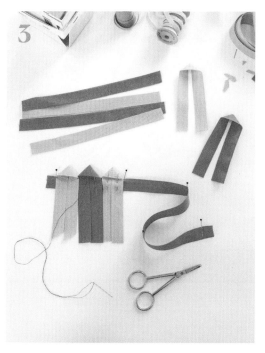

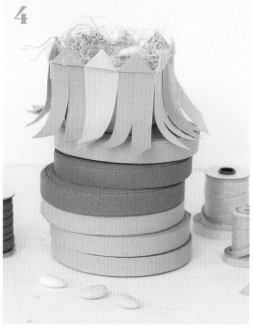

ONE Measure the length of the top rim of the basket. Cut a length of your ⅝-inch- (1.5 cm) wide ribbon, adding 1 inch (2.5 cm) to your measurement. (Our baskets are 15½ inches [39 cm] in circumference, so we cut 16½ inches [42 cm].)

TWO Lay the ribbon around the rim of the basket, marking where the ribbon meets each corner with a straight pin.

THREE Cut a total of twelve 8-inch (20 cm) lengths of ⅝-inch- (1.5 cm) wide ribbon. We used two different colors, so you'll need six pieces of ribbon in each color.

Next, take one piece of ribbon and fold it in half, allowing for a triangle to form at the center, or top, of the folded ribbon (as pictured). Next, pin the folded ribbon onto the longer ribbon, matching the bottom line of the triangle with the top edge of the ribbon, so that the left side of the bottom of the triangle meets at a corner pin. Ensure the inside edges of the piece stay together. Repeat with all remaining pieces.

FOUR Hand-stitch all pieces in place at sides and centers. Trim the ends of each ribbon piece at an angle to prevent fraying.

Paint the top edge of the basket with glue. Match your corner pins with the corners of the basket and glue them in place, making sure all corners meet.

Once you've wrapped the ribbon all the way around the rim, tuck any excess ribbon underneath with a dot of glue.

Fill with excelsior and Easter goodies. Enjoy!

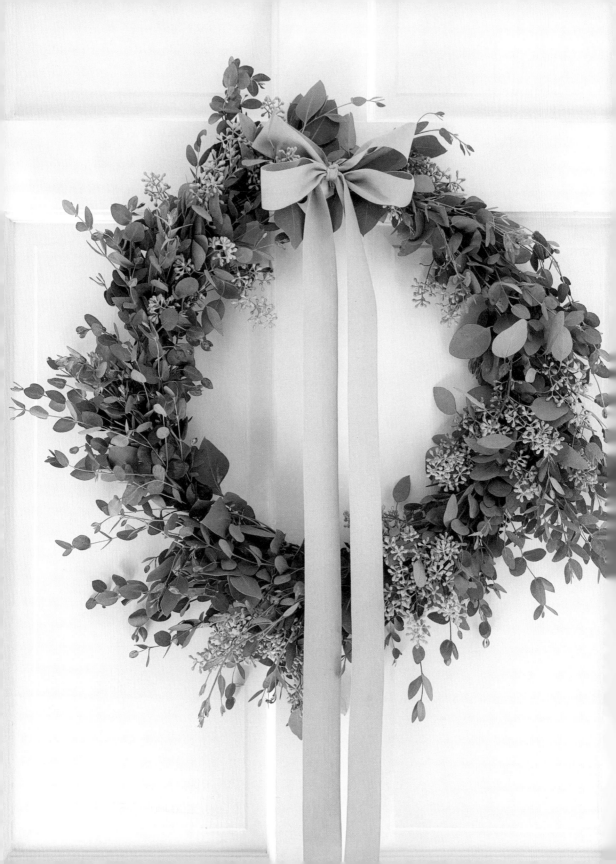

Wreaths

Wreaths are welcome decor for every door, any time of year—outside or inside. Trim with seasonal greens and top with your favorite ribbon.

SUPPLIES

Seasonal greens

Floral clippers

Wire cutter

Store-bought wire wreath or 24- or 22-gauge floral wire, cut to the circumference of your choice, usually 18 to 22 inches (46 to 56 cm)

Fine-gauge floral wire

Ribbon, 1½-inch (4 cm) wide and about 1 yard (91 cm) long

ONE Form the strong floral wire into a wreath shape.

TWO Tie the seasonal greenery into individual bundles with floral wire, then adhere onto the floral wire wreath frame with more floral wire.

THREE Wrap the ribbon around the top of the wreath and tie into a decorative bow, as show at left. Hang on your door or mantel, or wherever you wish!

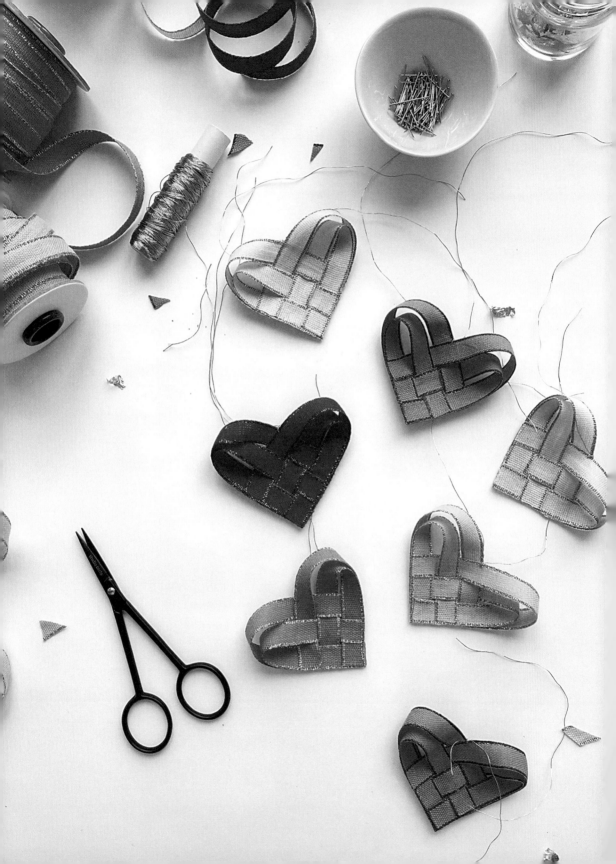

Valentine Hearts

These sweet woven hearts use Studio Carta's Drittofilo cotton ribbon and can double as ornaments or gift toppers, or they can be slipped into an envelope and mailed to loved ones near and far. These personalized decorative delicacies lend themselves to a rainbow of colors of your choosing. Play around with color combinations to inspire your creativity and garner the affection of friends and family.

SUPPLIES

Scissors

⅜-inch- (10 mm) wide ribbon

Craft glue

Gold metallic thread

Sewing needle

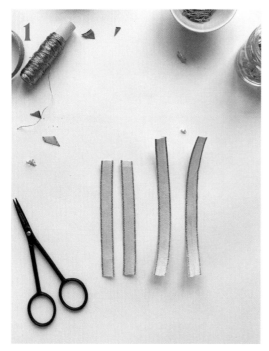

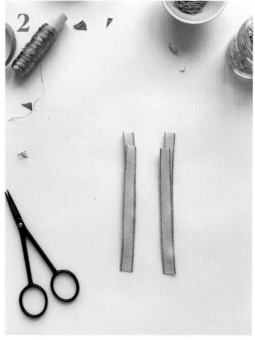

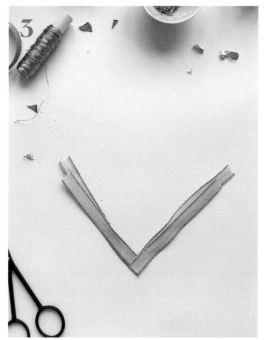

ONE Cut four pieces of ribbon: two measuring 4 inches (10 cm) and two measuring 4½ inches (11.5 cm).

TWO Layer the shorter piece of ribbon on top of the longer piece of ribbon by aligning the bottom edges. Secure with a dot of glue.

THREE Create a V by stacking one of the layered ribbon pieces on top of the other, ensuring the bottom glued edges are aligned to form a 90-degree angle. Secure with a dot of glue.

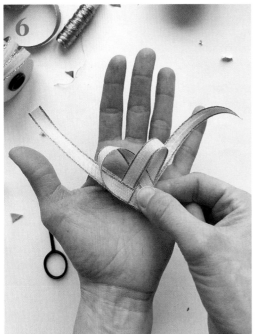

FOUR Fold the shorter front ribbon on the left side down to create a space to tuck in the shorter piece from the right side. Secure with a dot of glue, then fold the left side back upward.

FIVE Take the shorter piece from the left side and feed it through the loop on the right side (to create a pretzel shape). Secure with a dot of glue (ensuring edges are aligned).

SIX Take the longer piece from the right side and feed it through the loop on the left side. Secure with a dot of glue (ensuring edges are aligned). You will also want to add a dot of glue between the bottom two layers.

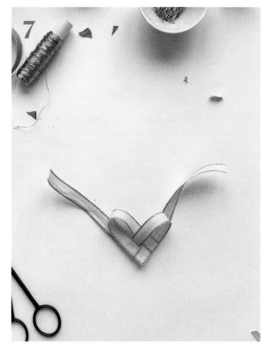

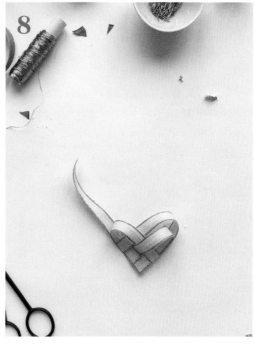

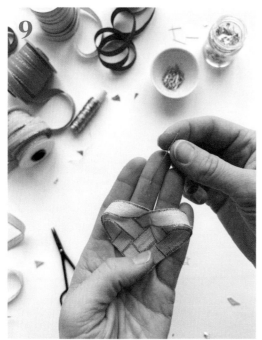

SEVEN To complete the heart, repeat step 6, this time left to right, making sure you weave the ribbon over and under so your last piece of ribbon rests between the two layers of ribbon on the right.

EIGHT Secure with a dot of glue.

NINE Adding thread for hanging: Thread a sharp needle with 12 inches (30.5 cm) of metallic thread. Push the needle through the two layers at the center of the ribbon heart, making sure all pieces align before pulling your thread through. Remove the needle and knot the thread to secure the two ribbon layers together. Knot ends to form a loop for hanging.

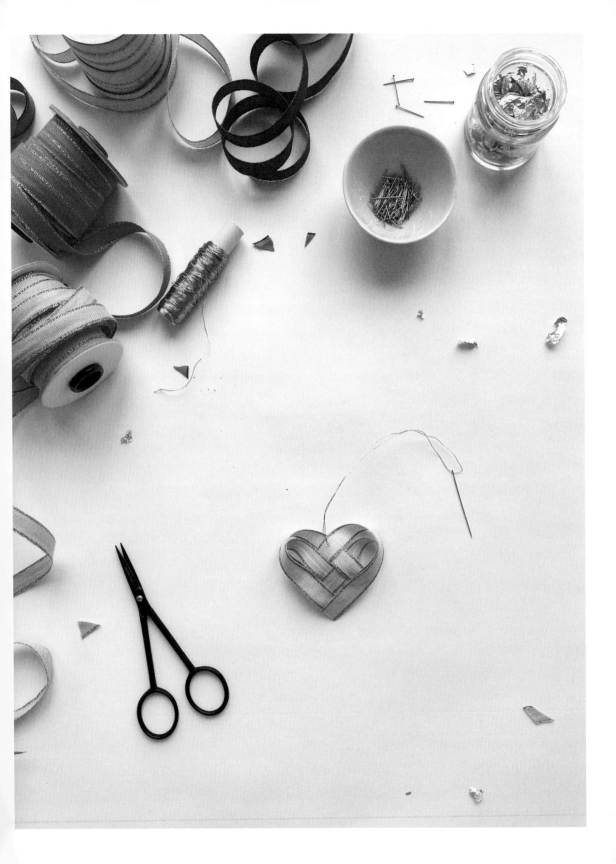

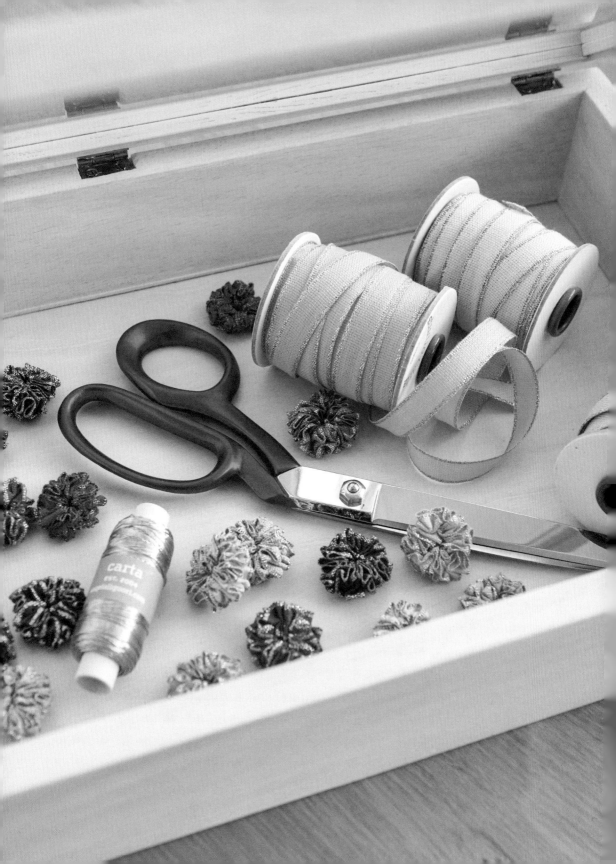

Ribbon-Flower Jewelry

While ribbons are most often used for gift wrapping, you can also use them to create a simple flower. For this project, designer Maria Picci transformed loose weave cotton ribbon into pretty pieces to wear. The flower is easy to make and requires few materials. No previous experience needed.

SUPPLIES

Loose weave cotton ribbon, ⅜ inch wide (10 mm), 18 inches long (45 cm)

Clear nylon monofilament thread

Sewing needle

Scissors

Hot glue gun and glue sticks

Ruler

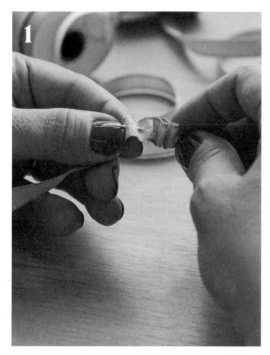

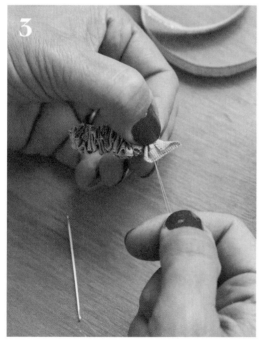

ONE Thread the needle with a double thread. Ensure that the length of the thread is manageable and not too long so that you avoid it getting knotted and are able to work comfortably. Cut the ribbon to the correct length. Begin by doubling over the end of the ribbon as shown and then sew along the center of the ribbon with stitches roughly ⅕ inch (½ cm) apart until you reach the end of the ribbon.

TWO As you stitch, slowly and carefully ruffle the ribbon, being careful not to overly tense the ribbon.

THREE Ruffle the entire length of ribbon, as shown. Next, stitch or glue the two ends of the ruffled ribbon together.

FOUR Your flower has blossomed!

FIVE Your finished flower can now be used in countless different projects! If you want to make a ring, glue or stitch the flower to a loop of wire or elastic as shown.

SIX Or be creative and make flower stick pins.

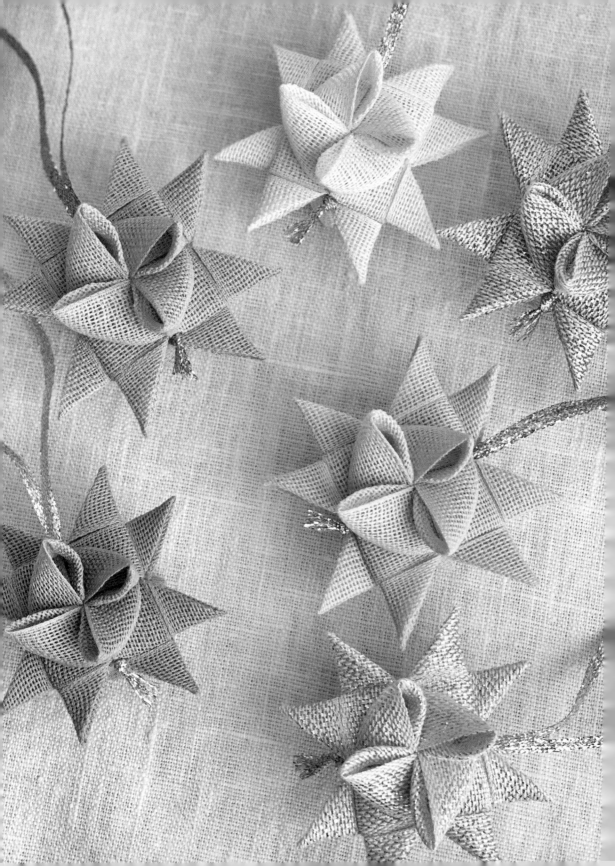

Nordic Stars

Nordic Stars have their roots in Germany, Denmark, and Sweden. Traditionally made with four strips of paper, here designer Lily Reid makes them with ribbon. Loose weave cotton ribbon, which is lightly starched, is perfect for the tight folds needed— and once you get the rhythm of making them, it's hard to stop. They look beautiful as ornaments, garlands, gift toppers— or rings and earrings!

SUPPLIES

Sharp scissors

Four 17-inch (43 cm) pieces of stiff ½-inch- (13 mm) wide Studio Carta Loose Weave Cotton Ribbon

Large-eye darning needle (#13 tapestry needle is best)

Note: We recommend starting to learn the folding involved in Nordic Stars with paper (the traditional material). It is less precious than your nice ribbons! You can make these stars any size depending on the width of the material you have. The narrower the ribbon, the shorter the strips; the wider the ribbon, the longer the strips. Make sure all strips are a uniform width. You can use any type of material, though a stiff, starched ribbon or paper holds the fold.

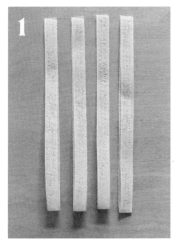

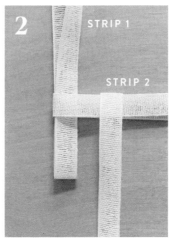

STRIP 1

STRIP 2

ONE Fold each strip in half. Make sure to crease the folds with your fingers so everything stays in place. If you want your points to be extra sharp, leave a small gap where the ribbon is folded double, to create the point.

TWO Weave the four strips together. Both ends of strip 1 should be in between strip 2.

THREE Scoot the strips together to tighten the central square.

FOUR Fold the top-left strip down. Fold the left strip to the right. Fold the bottom-right strip up. Finally, fold the top-right strip to the left.

FIVE This is how it should look.

SIX Weave this last strip under the layer made in the beginning of step 4.

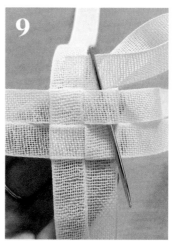

SEVEN Fold the top-right strip behind and toward the right. Make a 45-degree sharp crease.

EIGHT Fold the same strip down so it is adjacent to its original location and make a sharp 45-degree crease. Fold this strip to the left so it lies on top of itself.

NINE Grasp the point firmly, then weave with the needle the tail end of the strip under the layer just below it.

TEN Rotate the ribbon a quarter turn clockwise.

ELEVEN Repeat step 9 three more times.

TWELVE When completing the last strip, you will need to lift a strip out of the way to weave in the last strip. When done, it should look like this.

THIRTEEN Flip the entire model bottom-side up.

FOURTEEN Repeat steps 9 through 13. When trimming the ends make sure not to cut your folded part of the star!

FIFTEEN Now, you are ready to make the four peaks, or star points, by rearranging the strips of ribbon. You can fold the star points in any order. Once you fold a strip into a star point, tuck the end into a woven strip.

SIXTEEN You can flip the piece over to make a point with that strip. Keeping this rule in mind will mean that making the points is easy.

SEVENTEEN Fold the top-right strip away from the center, making a 45-degree-angle fold as shown. Crease the fold with your fingernail.

EIGHTEEN Fold the strip down, making a nice sharp point. Use your fingernail to crease the fold.

NINETEEN Fold the point in half onto itself, with the end of the strip lying over the opposite strip. Gently tuck the end of the strip under the opposite strip.

TWENTY Pull the strip through tightly, so that when you let go it will be hidden underneath.

TWENTY-ONE Cut off and discard about an inch of ribbon.

TWENTY-TWO Your Nordic Star!

TWENTY-THREE To thread a ribbon hanging loop through, double knot the end of a loop of thin ribbon or twine about twelve inches long.

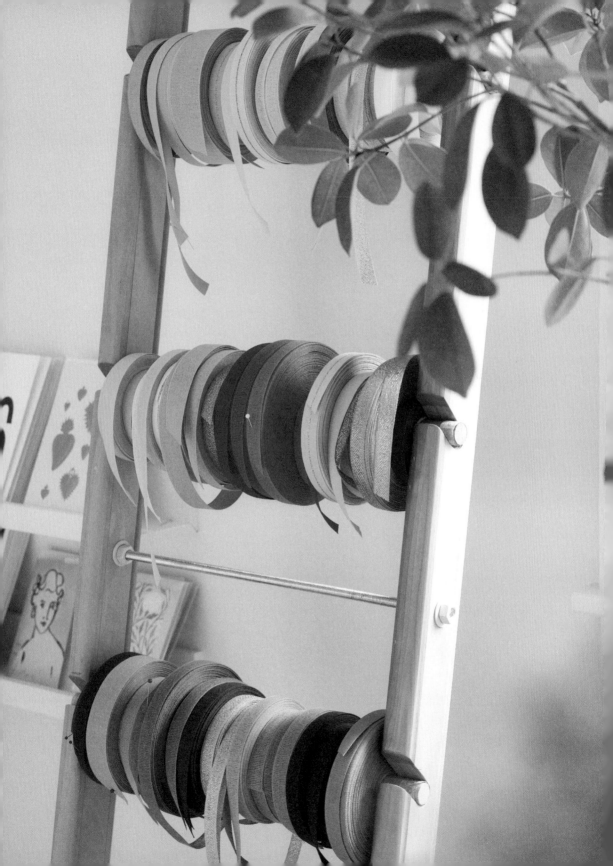

ANGELA LIGUORI AND THE STUDIO CARTA STORY

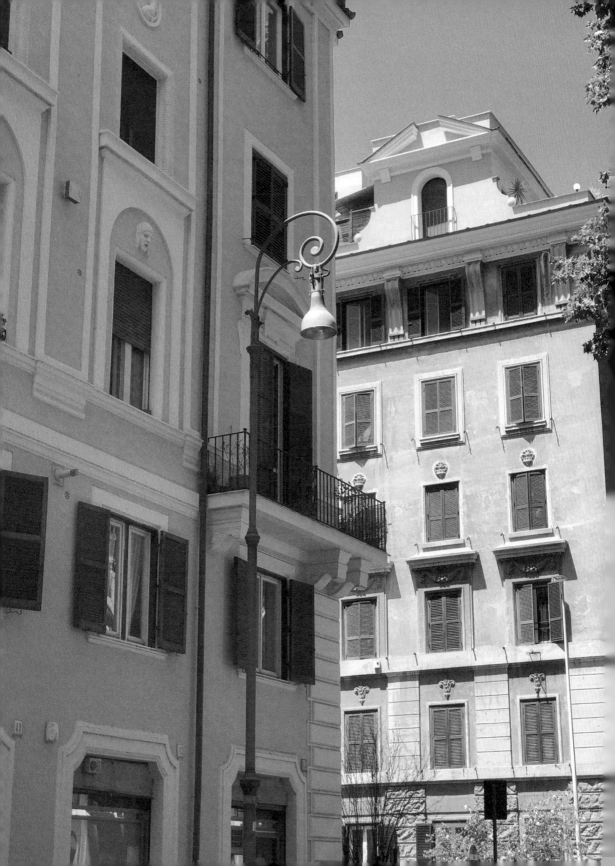

Weaving Memories, Honoring the Past, Community, and Italian-Made Craft

What does it take to transform an idea into reality? What kind of spirit and inspiration do dreams need to flourish in today's world? From her modest childhood in Rome, to building a trusted craft brand known across the globe, how did Angela Liguori bring the unrivalled Studio Carta to life? It all reads like a dream from the start to now, but like many great stories, we have to go back to the beginning to uncover the stepping-stones and hidden lessons that contributed to the artist and entrepreneur that Angela is today. This tale is a true one.

ITALIAN HERITAGE

Like most cities in Italy, Rome spools from the city center. Worn cobblestone roads weave into sprawling piazzas anchored with fountains. Intricate frescoes and marbled archways from centuries past decorate buildings patinated with the various hues of Italian life. Near that center lies the Vatican, and not too far from there, a modest apartment facing south gazes toward Michelangelo's Dome of St. Peter's.

The Rome building at Piazza Giovine Italia, 7, where Angela grew up. The building is still the same, and the color and the piazza's quiet atmosphere remain as she remembers them. The majestic Vatican is just a few blocks away.

If you were to pass by this apartment sometime in the mid-1970s, you might have heard a dressmaker cutting fabric with her sharp, sturdy scissors, her sewing machine humming alongside the flap of pigeons taking flight. You might have heard the rustle of a newspaper being leafed through by a retired naval officer, waiting for his daughter to make her next checkers move. In this apartment, near the center of Rome, you might see a young Angela Liguori staring dreamily out of the windows, engulfed with the view of the Cupola di San Pietro, the shades of the travertine stone changing with every passing hour. The dome is sometimes a greyish olive at dusk, a bright blush in the midday sun, or a dusty ochre at golden hour. The sky, the landscape, and the buildings of Rome are never one color. The city is a kaleidoscope of pigments, which come alive at every breaking of the clouds, or at each new ray of sunlight that emerges from them. These are the views that Angela Liguori grew up with, and in many ways, they also reflect the story of a celebrated shop she will create in twenty years' time: Studio Carta.

Today, Studio Carta is a haven for quality: desk and sewing accessories and Italian-made heirloom tools for craft-making, as well as ingenious greeting cards, stunning wrapping paper, and artful textiles by designers and stylists hand-selected by Angela. The Studio also hosts public workshops and events, featuring a handful of collaborative local artists. Studio Carta has become known for its cotton ribbons, exclusively made in Italy, the patterns and colors designed with Angela's signature style. Artfully presented, it is akin to walking into a gallery, each object resting in a myriad of vignettes. But in many ways, Studio Carta is intangible, and much more than the sum of its parts. The shop that Angela Liguori created is a community, a family, a feeling.

The photo of Angela (left) and her mother in summer 1996 is the only image of her mother sewing. The shelf holds Angela's calendar and specialty ribbons.

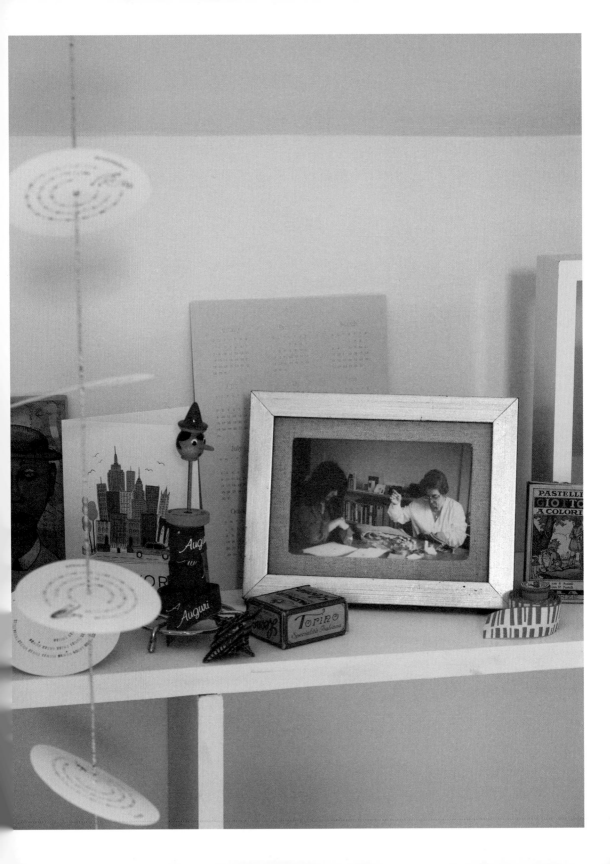

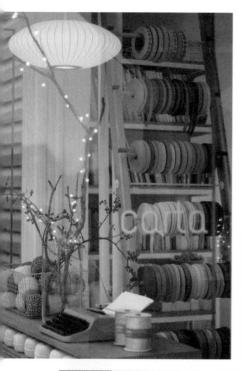

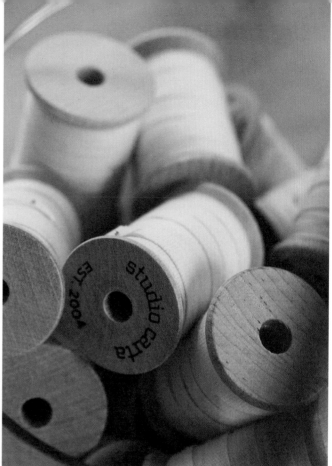

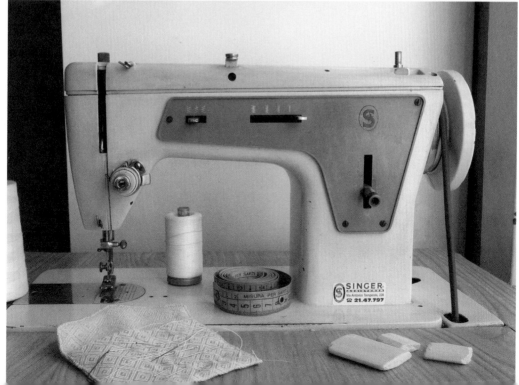

Angela Liguori was born in Rome in 1968, ten years after her older brothers. Even though the siblings shared a close bond, she enjoyed uninterrupted time with her mother and father as an "only" child. She took walks with her father through the winding Roman roads and, on special occasions, visited him at his office in the city. After eighteen years in the Navy, her father worked for the government as an auditor at the *Corte dei Conti* (the Court of Audit). Angela found herself in awe of each tool that he had somewhere on his dark wooden work desk: ornate stationery on Fabriano paper, inky pens, rubber stamps, an Olivetti typewriter that seemed larger than life. Mundane objects meant for everyday clerical tasks became enchanted once picked up by Angela's small hands. How incredible that these daily tools could be both the instruments of creation and, better yet, works of art.

The same type of alchemy appeared in her mother's toolkit, which unfurled from her sewing table in the Liguori's living room, nestled against the same windows facing St. Peter's Dome. Her open sewing box, bursting at the seams with needles, thread, and buttons, became young Angela's treasure hunt. The young girl sorted the wooden spools by thread color and marveled at the weight of the factory-grade scissors, larger than her own forearm. Could this be where Angela's passion for creating art began? One thing is for sure, her entrepreneurial spirit was absolutely passed down. Before her mother had children, she had seven seamstresses working under her. In post-World War II Naples, this was a feat on its own. Even after the traditions of southern Italian life called on Angela's mother to stay home and focus on the family, she remained hardworking as ever, sewing for clients between housework, providing opportunities for her children and, perhaps without knowing it, a roadmap for her daughter to follow.

Clockwise from top left: Studio Carta's original Brookline, Massachusetts, shop, with spools of ribbon and Angela's typewriter, in honor of her father's vintage Olivetti; Studio Carta spools; the Singer sewing machine was her mother's companion for life, living in the Liguoris' home in Rome. Years after her mother passed, spools of thread, the measuring tape, and her needles remain.

Angela was passionate about art from a young age, and it blossomed at every milestone, in every corner of Italy she explored. She was surrounded by some of the most stunning ancient Roman, Renaissance, baroque, and modern art in the world. The colors and textures of Rome and its neighboring towns were seeping into each new creative venture she took. Baroque buildings and Italian frescoes from the sixteenth to seventeenth centuries started to paint the palette in her mind of something to come. But it wasn't the landscape alone. The catalytic element of influential people brought her ideas to life. Take, for instance, a chance meeting with fellow artist Silvana Amato, a teenager four years older than Angela (ages eighteen and fourteen, respectively). Silvana's family lived beneath the Liguori's apartment. One afternoon, Silvana found and admired some of Angela's René Magritte postcards that were scattered on her bedroom desk. From that moment, they grew up to become longtime collaborators. In fact, their limited-edition calendars, which were some of the first to come out of Studio Carta, were created in collaboration. Together, they went on to produce more than ten years of collaborative book art, starting in 1998. Angela's passion might have started when she was in middle school and her twenty-two-year-old brother brought her a gift of stationery from southern France. More than just paper, it was sumptuous, Parisian laid paper with subtle gradients, unlike anything Angela had seen or felt before. This led her to experiment with other paper art forms, such as marbling. Soon, she was hand-marbling her own stationery sets, a practice that has been refined in Italy since the sixteenth century. Eager to learn, Angela looked around to apprentice with Italian masters but quickly found that many of them were secretive and protective of their processes. Discovering that many European artists concealed their methods was pivotal to Angela's future search for community and collaboration, in a new country five-thousand miles across the sea.

Fontana del Nettuno is one of the three fountains in Piazza Navona designed by architect and sculptor Giacomo della Porta in 1574. He also created St. Peter's Basilica. Piazza Navona, a large square surrounded by narrow streets and hidden churches, is one of Angela's favorite destinations in Rome.

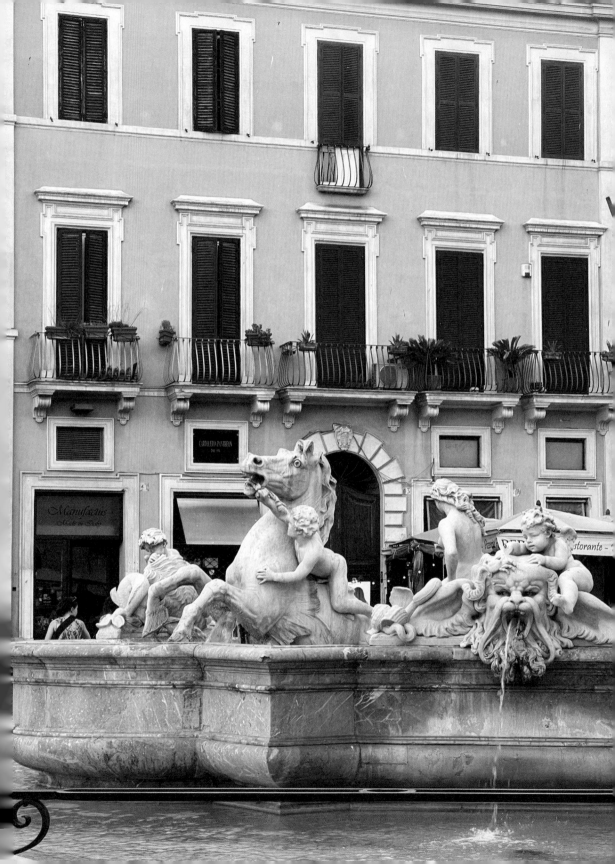

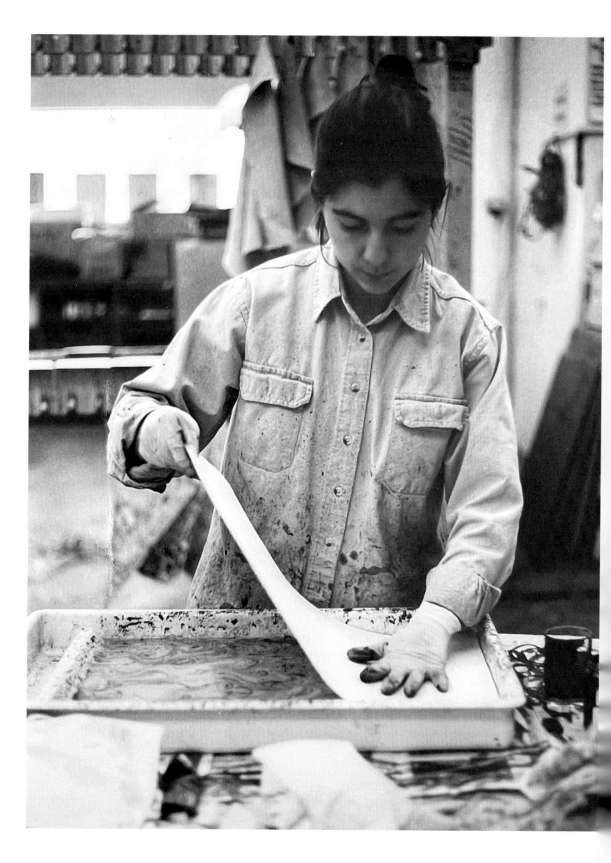

ANGELA'S CREATIVE TOOLKIT:
PAPER AND BOOK ARTS

The young artist kept developing on her own, paper marbling and experimenting everywhere she could lay her trays out, like on her parent's balcony. By late high school, Angela was putting together her own unique stationery sets for her friends. Her exposure to more artistic pathways only multiplied. During her last year of high school, Angela found an internship at a graphic design studio right beside the Pantheon. Meanwhile, her older cousin urged her to visit the University of Bologna, where she studied. Soon enough, Angela was studying art history at the oldest university in the world, basking in the streets of the ancient town, and selling her marbled paper stationery sets in the art markets of the medieval squares. While in Bologna, a friend told her about a bookbinding course taught by Giovanni Vecchi, the owner of the workshop and store Il Cartiglio. Angela jumped at the chance, and soon was working part-time for Giovanni, learning traditional bookbinding while studying and completing her degree. The tiny bookbinding boutique employed a handful of other crafters who made photo albums, journals, boxes, and stationery showcasing Giovanni's marble papers. When they were finished crafting a piece in the back studio, they only needed to walk a few feet to the large windows facing Via San Carlo to display Giovanni's unique marbled papers and paper goods. In addition to her work for Giovanni, Angela was offered a small space and the studio's equipment to make her own marbled paper products: tools and a table to cut heavy board to make journals and photo albums that she sold in the medieval Le Due Torri square, a monthly arts-and-crafts market that extended to two weeks during the holidays. Perhaps it was here that ignited another idea for Angela: a studio where artists worked, collaborated, and showcased in one place.

Studio Carta could have been born in any of these moments. Angela isn't convinced her company grew from a single seed or a single place. With the gift of retrospect, we at least can be certain that the many seeds of Studio Carta were firmly planted in all of these places.

Opposite: Angela in 1994, marbling paper at the Minnesota Center for Book Arts, Minneapolis. As an intern at MCBA at the time, she marbled paper once a week in the papermaking studio, where she was also responsible for organizing the space before workshops—in exchange for her using the space for her own projects.

Below: The curved needle used by bookbinding artist Bari Zaki during a link stitch workshop at Studio Carta.

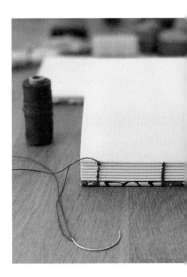

JOURNEY TO THE UNITED STATES

It was a leap of faith and a plane ticket to the United States that started to germinate and form roots of Studio Carta. Angela found herself at Lunalux in Minneapolis, one of the rare American design studios that was reviving the art of letterpress printing in the 1990s. Realizing that the market for cards in the United States was much larger than Italy, Angela started showing her marbled paper stationery to shop owners. They bought bundles on the spot. At that time, there was another renaissance happening for book arts, and Angela just happened to be at the center of it. During a transformative period from 1994 to 1997, Angela worked as the assistant of Bridget O'Malley (co-founder of Cave Paper) at the Minnesota Center for Book Arts. In her final year there, she was the esteemed artist-in-residence, following in O'Malley's footsteps. For the first time in years, Angela wasn't creating alone, but with an expanded community of artists and fellows who shared in a collaborative spirit she hadn't felt until then. Angela traveled to Taos, New Mexico to meet and work with Polly Fox, a paper-marbling revivalist and founder of *Ink & Gall*, a magazine specializing in the art of marbling, and then Fulbright scholar Tim Barrett, known for his papermaking research in Japan. Angela secured an internship at the University of Iowa's Center for the Book, where she studied with Barrett. She also landed a prestigious three-month summer internship at the Women's Studio Workshop in Rosendale, New York, under the stewardship of Ann Kalmbach and Tatana Kellner, expert book artists who ran and taught the papermaking, printing, and bookbinding workshops. While supporting herself by selling her own marbled paper products to several shops around the United States, Angela assisted with book and paper artists traveling to the Women's Studio to teach.

Her creative toolkit was sharpened and expanded at every turn, all the while mastering English as a second language. Perhaps it was the universality of numbers and dates while learning a difficult language that developed Angela's fondness for calendar art. Reenter childhood friend Silvana Amato. Together, she and Angela crafted intricately bound calendars and limited-edition books under the imprint of Edizioni Almenodue (Press of at Least Two), with unique designs both ahead of their time and rooted in history. Just as she did as a child, Angela continued to peruse the aisles of specialty bookshops and adore how the exquisite, paper-bound books felt in her hands. It was time, she thought, to graduate from consumer to creator, finally adding her work to the shelves of art history.

Above: A limited edition book that Angela designed in collaboration with Silvana Amato (with illustrations by Rita Ravaioli).

Opposite, clockwise from top left: Angela teaching marbled paper workshop in Ann Arbor, Michigan; hand-bound books made by Angela; "Calendarbook" designed "by Angela and Silvana, 2013; marbling paper demo at a Wood Engravers Network meeting in Ann Arbor; Angela's bookbinding supplies.

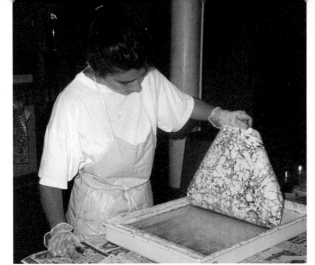

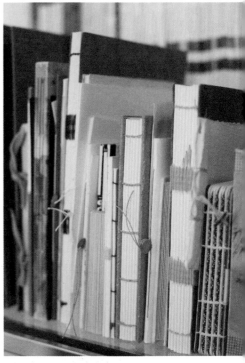

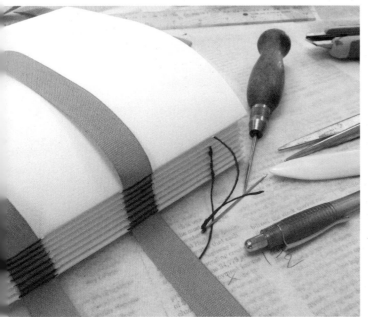

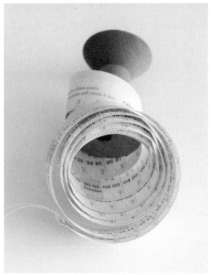

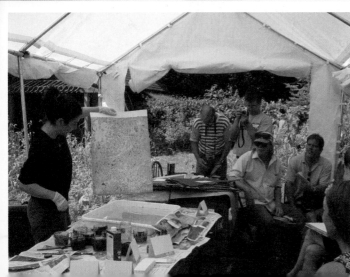

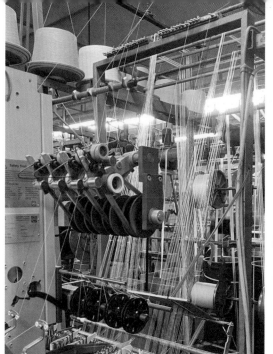
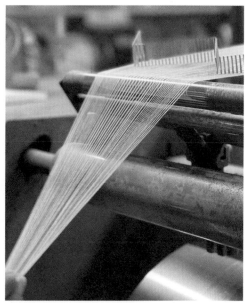
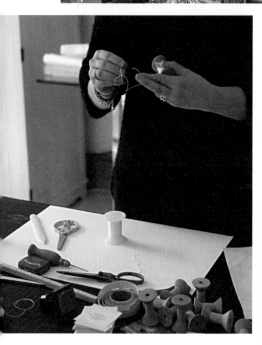
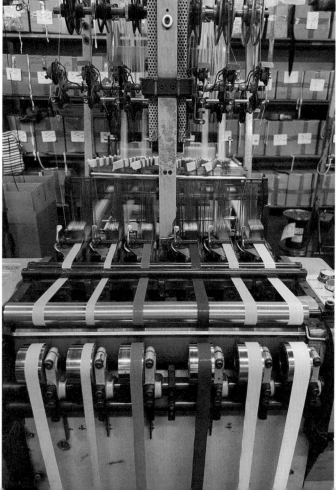

ANGELA'S ENTREPRENEURIAL SPIRIT: STUDIO CARTA IS BORN

In 1997, Angela returned to Italy after three intensive years abroad. She recalls being brought to tears rediscovering the beauty of the land she left behind. It was in this tender space, while reuniting with her homeland, that she met and married Mohamed Alaeddin, a Syrian dental student. Then, work brought him to Michigan in the United States, where Angela took another chance to see where her skills might take her. For the next seven years, while she raised three children, from newborn to toddler-aged, Angela taught book arts at Hollander's in Ann Arbor. On the weekends, Mohamed looked after the children while she continued to teach workshops. There, Angela honed her skills on the business side of the industry. She was a natural, the entrepreneurial spirit alive. She started to sell her creations at trunk shows from the renowned paper shop and soon she had a renewed sense of how to create, produce, and market a line of products.

DESIGNING STUDIO CARTA RIBBONS AND ACCESSORIES

The biggest breakthrough for Studio Carta happened in the discovery of a simple detail, after a simple request. Along the spine of her hand bound books was a tightly woven Italian cotton ribbon. Angela also styled her table displays with stacks of these ribbon spools. Clients and customers were asking if they could buy just the ribbon, a luxe cotton weave that they'd never seen or felt before. Realizing there was nothing else like it in the country, Angela called her mother right away and asked her to do some detective work back home. Before they knew it, they had the top secret contact of the manufacturer. It was one of the last gifts Angela's mother gave to her before she passed away. In 2008, Angela recalls feeling mixed emotions—excitement, fear, and strength—when she placed her first official ribbon order with the factory. To this day, Angela produces—and now designs—Studio Carta ribbons with the same manufacturer her mother introduced to her.

Opposite, clockwise from top left: Three different machines in action at the cotton ribbon factory in Italy; Angela making ribbon spools in the studio.

Above: Mohamed with their firstborn and eldest son, Hani, visiting a letterpress printing studio in Ann Arbor.

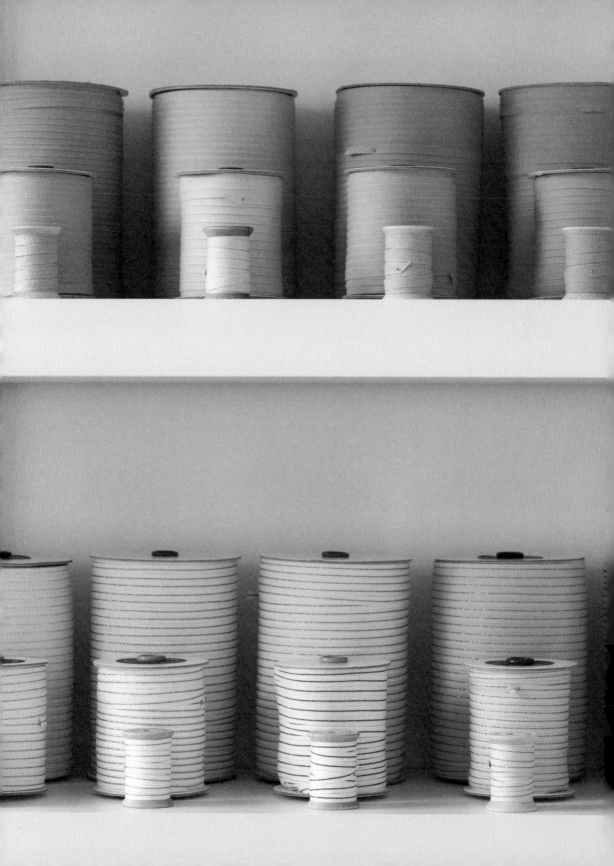

In 2006, Mohamed accepted a teaching position at Boston University, and the family of five moved to the New England hub, where Angela continued to produce a wildly popular run of calendars, limited edition books, and paper goods in collaboration with multiple artists, while continuing to teach book arts workshops. In 2010, she breathed new life into Studio Carta with a brick-and-mortar shop in Brookline, Massachusetts. Now with school-aged children, Angela had six fleeting hours each day during the week to dedicate to her brand. She spent the time at her studio, dreaming of the next new line and growing the business.

With her family, Angela has been traveling back to Italy multiple times a year, scouting new products, exclusively made in Italy, and mostly creating new color stories for ribbons based on the Italian streets and landscapes that fostered her creative pursuits. In a way, she can now capture the frescoes and carvings of her past and share them with the world. Inspired by the winding streets and skies back home, Angela crafts her own colors for her ribbons. Color stories are born from the hues of those places that were so formative to her. Each ribbon shade is signature Studio Carta, exclusively made with the Italian manufacturer. Just to highlight a few:

Opposite: Studio Carta ribbons.

Above: Angela and Mohamed at their original Brookline ribbon studio.

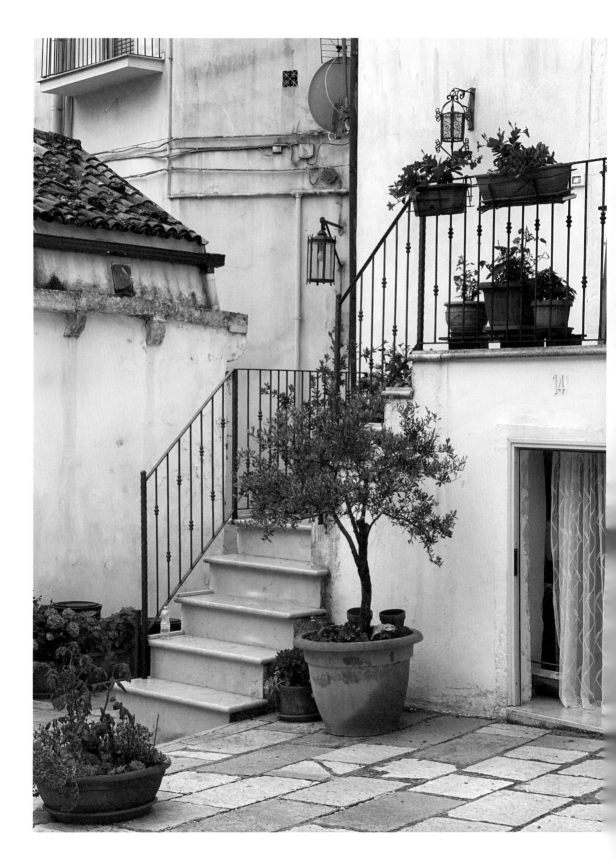

olive

There is the soft and versatile Olive, inspired by a visit to Puglia. The earthen shade peeps beneath stones on the road, and olive trees dot almost every vista.

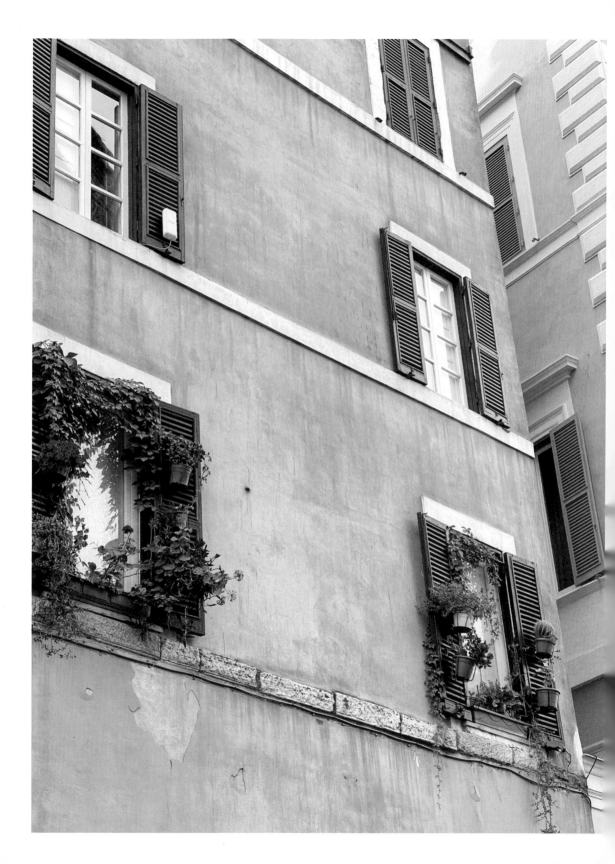

blush

Plucked from Angela's hometown of Rome, there's Blush, a buffed rose inspired by the worn stone walls that glow a subtle pink against a row of black shutters.

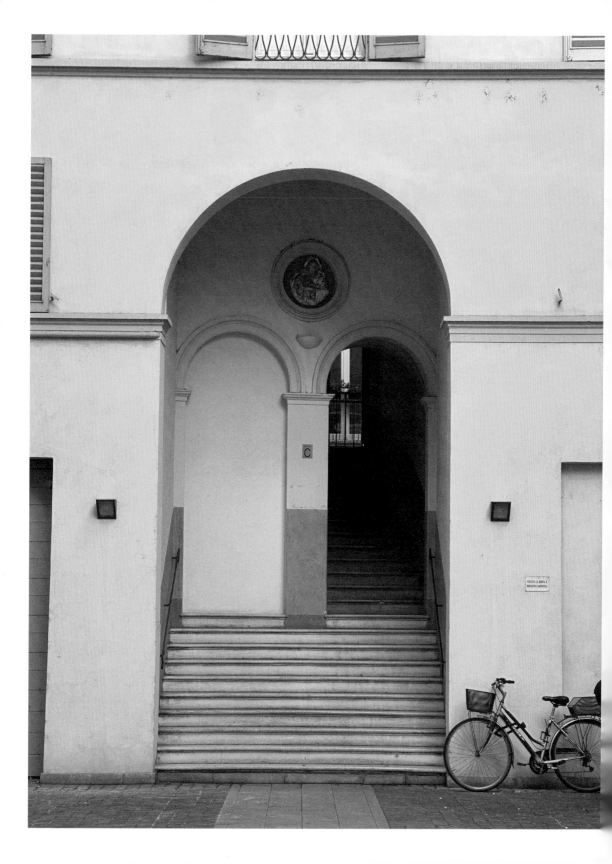

ochre

And Ochre is pulled from Angela's beloved Bologna. This rich golden hue comes alive with each sunset and sunrise she bathed in along the ancient roads that taught her how to see, once upon a time.

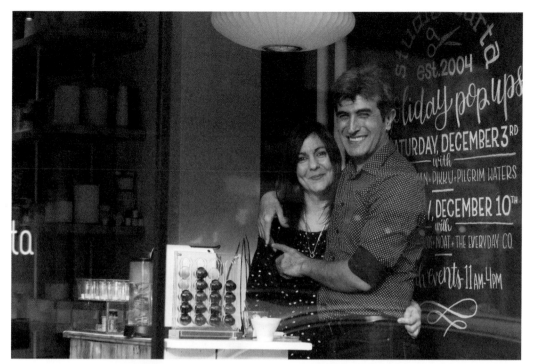

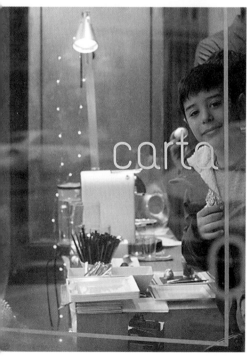

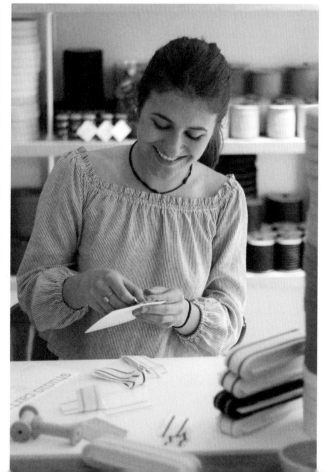

BUILDING COMMUNITY
AND COLLABORATION

Studio Carta's latest evolution is its Chestnut Hill headquarters, where Angela and Mohamed moved in 2021, a leafy, quiet neighborhood just outside of Boston. As of today, she has hosted many memorable in-person workshops and events there, as well as worldwide virtual studio tours.

At the heart of Studio Carta lies a desire to share craft and wisdom with the community, a generous angle that Angela found lacking in Italy all those years ago when masters shrouded their skills in secrecy. Now, a master herself, Angela is at home in her light-filled studio working on her next pieces or coordinating her next workshop, excited to share her wisdom with everyone. Sweeping white walls are anchored with the original wooden beams aloft. Spools of ribbon in all sizes are arranged in thematic ombrés across the shelves. Her mother's scissors sit in tableau for visitors to view. Curated Italian crafts and tools dot the room, acting as modern takes on her father's desk. All of these items form a shimmering mosaic, as they become dappled with afternoon sun peeking through the canopy of trees above. Studio Carta is not one color, it's an ever-changing tapestry of Angela's life come alive.

You can hear it when you're here, Angela's entire family immersed in some way, as her three children have done since an early age. Listen closely on any given day and you might hear her daughter Nadá, now in her early twenties and living in Italy, talking with clients, taking orders, and offering marketing ideas for Studio Carta. Each year, Nadá returns to the States to lend a hand and her lifelong expertise at Shoppe Object, the big New York trade show. Or her son Hani, who assembles and packages products, carefully inspecting quality control on each product before Mohamed packs a big order. Or, you might hear Nael, Studio Carta's fashion and styling advisor, giving Angela some advice and feedback on a new product launch. When Mohamed's not teaching at Harvard Dental School, you'll probably detect the aroma from one of the signature espresso macchiatos he is preparing for visitors. In the small, but dedicated, Studio team, everyone lends a hand at the shop and the trade shows.

Family members are all very much a part of Studio Carta, past and present.

Opposite and above: Angela, Mohamed, and their children at the Brookline studio.

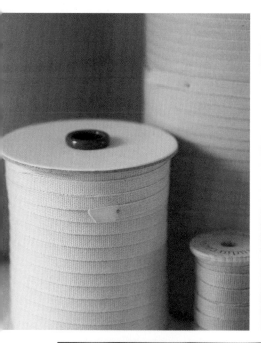

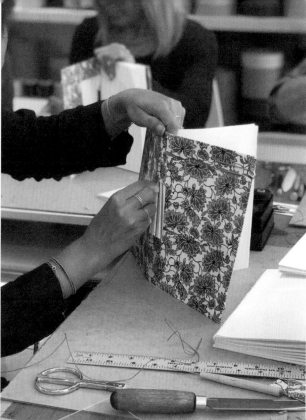

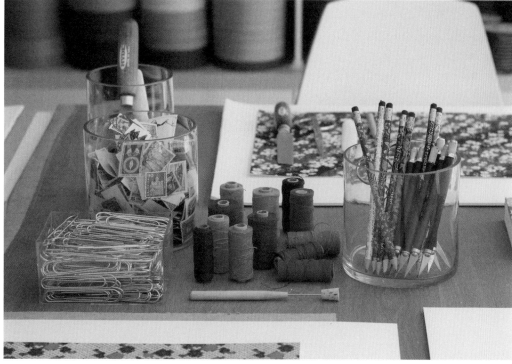

At one of Angela's collaborative events, you might hear the sounds of laughter and discussion, with music playing softly in the background. A full circle sense of history brings up emotion in Angela, so moved to see her kids work alongside her and Mohamed. Together, the gifts and lessons they pass down to their children are ever-evolving. But there is one beautiful (and rare) takeaway that rises to the top of this journey: that an artistic life can support a family with enough hard work, resilience, and dedication. It's the life that her mother might not have exactly had all those years ago, but the one that she envisioned for Angela. Today, if you look through the windows of Studio Carta, you might see everything it has become.

—Coco McCracken

STUDIO CARTA

501 Heath Street
Chestnut Hill, MA 02467

info@studiocartashop.com

Opposite, clockwise from top left: Studio Carta ribbon; details of the long-stitch bookbinding workshop hosted at the Studio Carta studio, taught by Chicago-based bookbinder Bari Zaki; Studio Carta's newly crafted vintage desk supplies.

Above: Angela, captured by photographer Justine Hand while shooting a DIY project.

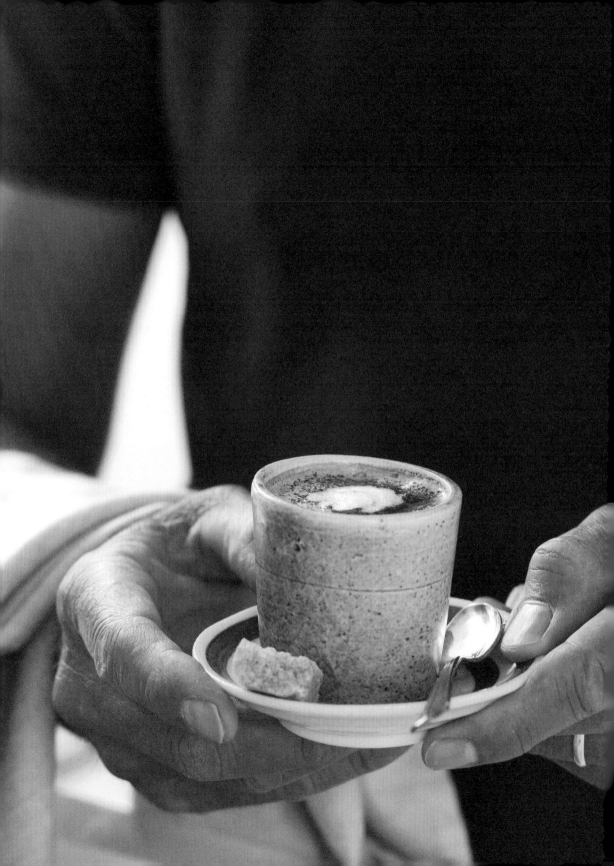

Espresso Macchiato

Espresso is a favorite treat both in Italy and at the Studio Carta US headquarters in Chestnut Hill, Massachusetts. At the Studio, customers clamor for Mohamed's version, which is served all day at the shop. Here, he shares his recipe for authentic espresso macchiato you can make at home. Enjoy some after completing one of the wrapping or ribbon projects in this book!

INGREDIENTS

One sugar cube (cane sugar if possible) or granulated sugar to taste

One serving of your favorite espresso (We use a Nespresso machine at the studio, but traditionally prepared espresso, or even a stovetop moka pot, will work, too.)

Cocoa powder

Steamed foamed milk, served very hot (If you do not have a milk steamer, warm the milk gently in a pan until hot but not boiling.)

Mohamed Alaeddin's espresso macchiato.

ONE Always place the sugar in the cup first; a cube of cane sugar is best.

TWO Pour the prepared espresso over the sugar in the cup, leaving some room at the top, then finish with a sprinkle of the cocoa powder on top of the espresso, then a topping of foamed milk.

THREE Always serve with a plate and a spoon. (Never miss these details!) Add a chocolate to the plate to eat after the espresso; it is the best combo.

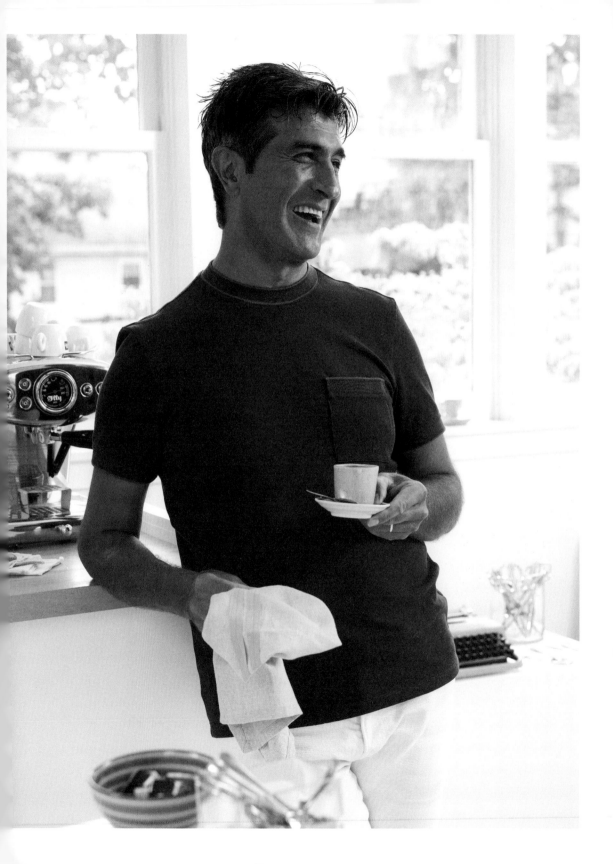

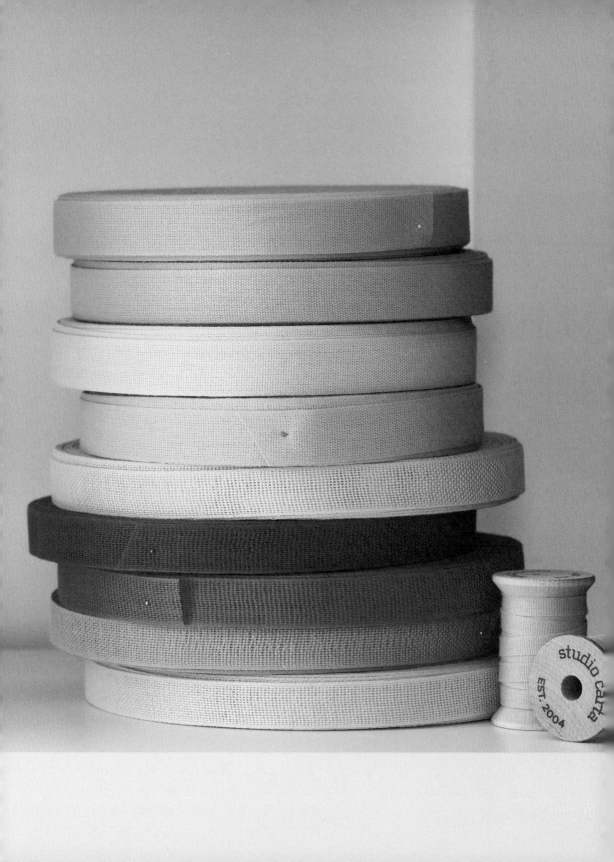

SHOP, DECORATE, EAT, ENJOY!

Throughout the year, Angela Liguori frequently collaborates with other designers, makers, and crafters: She loves to open Studio Carta's doors to host events and workshops. Some of the many studios Angela works with in the United States, Italy, and abroad are listed here, to offer you inspiration and ideas for making every part of life more beautiful.

MASSACHUSETTS AND THE UNITED STATES

ALBERTINE PRESS

1309 Cambridge Street, Cambridge, MA

A stationery, wedding invitation, and letterpress studio and shop.

www.albertinepress.com

APPRENTICE STUDIO

9591 Main Street, Penngrove, CA

A small knitwear and design studio located in the Petaluma, California area, owned by Lily Reid and specializing in women's and children's custom clothing. Lily created the Nordic Stars and kits (pages 124–29) with our line of cotton ribbon, to be used as holiday ornaments and gift toppers.

www.apprenticestudio.com

BARI ZAKI STUDIO

3858 North Lincoln Avenue, Chicago, IL

Fine bookbinding and workshops, with a unique collection of paper, desk accessories, and ribbon at Bari's studio and shop.

www.barizaki.com

BOSTON DESIGN SALON

A network for Boston's creative female entrepreneurs running businesses within the arts.

www.design-salon-index.squarespace.com

EM LETTERPRESS

25 Wareham Street, Unit 2A, Middleborough, MA

Elias Roustom has been running his printing studio for more than twenty years, and he is our favorite source for quality letterpress printing for all Studio Carta printing needs.

www.emletterpress.com

JILL ROSENWALD

369 Congress Street, Boston, MA

Pottery studio that is recognized for vibrant patterns and thoughtful color combinations, all designed and made in the Fort Point district of Boston.

www.jillrosenwald.com

KELLY HARRIS SMITH

Boston, MA

Kelly Harris Smith is a textile and product designer specializing in natural, sustainable, and recycled materials for commercial and residential interior design.

www.kellyharrissmith.com

LES FLEURS

27 Barnard Street, Andover, MA

High-end florist featuring fresh flower arrangements, plants, and French antiques.

www.lesfleurs.com

MAYBELLE IMASA-STUKULS

Calligrapher, artist, and author of *The Gift of Calligraphy: A Modern Approach to Hand Lettering with 25 Projects to Give and Keep.*

www.instagram.com/maybelleimasa/

MOONTREE LETTERPRESS

823 Sherers Hill Road, Riegelsville, PA

A letterpress studio specializing in personal stationery and wedding invitations. Designer and printer Rebecca Kutys takes pride in the quality of every finished project that leaves the studio.

www.moontreeletterpress.com

MOLLY SUBER THORPE

Lettering artist, calligraphy instructor, and author of multiple books about modern calligraphy and handwriting styles.

www.mollysuberthorpe.com

NOAT

Somerville, MA

Stationery and greeting cards designed and letterpress-printed in the Boston area.

www.noat.co

NORTH GARDEN AND GOODS

Exeter, NH

Founded in 2019 by Amanda Casey, North Garden and Goods was inspired by a lifelong love for all things flora. She cultivates beauty through flowers, one garden at a time.

www.north-nh.com

PILGRIMWATERS

Gloucester, MA

Susy and Keith are designers and makers with a modern handmade aesthetic. Susy's textiles range from cashmere scarves and throws to cotton/silk dresses. Each product is carefully designed, created, and produced by highly skilled artisanal manufacturers in India and Nepal. The one-of-a-kind functional furniture pieces are made by Keith, built from scratch in small batches in Gloucester, Massachusetts.

www.pilgrimwaters.co

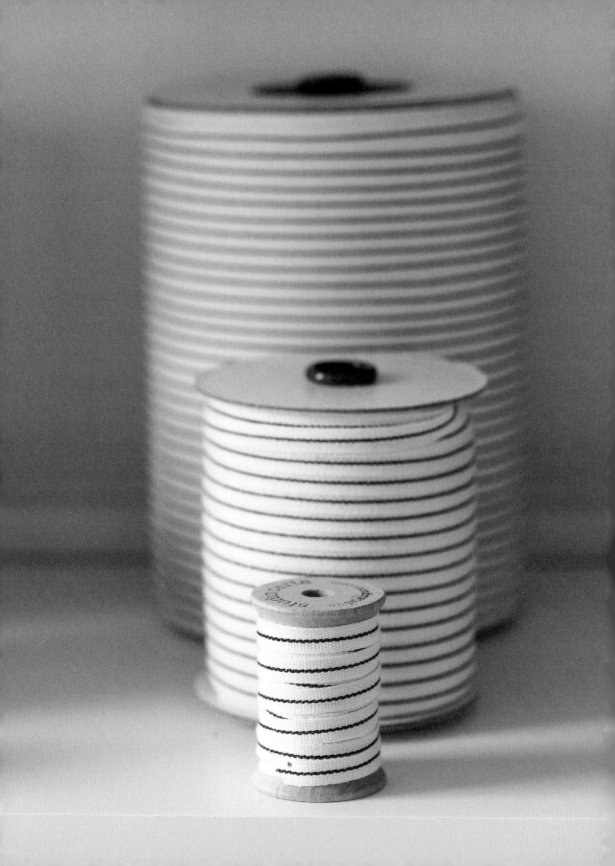

POD

35 Sacramento Street, Cambridge, MA

A tiny neighborhood boutique offering inspired simplicity. Pod is where Angela first exhibited her stationery and paper goods, when the family moved to Boston in 2006.

www.shop-pod.com

PURL SOHO

Santa Ana, CA

Excellent source for everything knitting and sewing. Purl Soho was the first shop in the United States to carry Studio Carta's first collection of cotton ribbon!

www.purlsoho.com

STITCH AND TICKLE

63 Thayer Street, Boston, MA

Small, independent lifestyle boutique located in the heart of SoWa in Boston. Sophie Truong designs handmade leather bags in her studio, right behind the shop.

www.stitchandtickle.com

THE HOUSE THAT LARS BUILT

Provo, UT

Craft and design daily-projects blog, established by Brittany Watson Jepsen, author of *Craft the Rainbow: 40 Colorful Paper Projects from The House That Lars Built*. The site has grown from one blogger, Brittany, in her apartment, to a creative team of seven, located in historic Provo, Utah.

www.thehousethatlarsbuilt.com

THUSS + FARRELL

New York

Thuss + Farrell is the multidisciplinary team of Rebecca Thuss and Patrick Farrell, based in New York and specializing in creative direction, photography, and design.

www.thussfarrell.com

ITALY AND BEYOND

ANONIMA IMPRESSORI

Via San Carlo 44–44a, Bologna, Italy

Anonima Impressori is a graphic- and fine letterpress–printing workshop in the heart of medieval Bologna, established by Veronica Bassini, Luca Lattuga, and Massimo Pastore. They specialize in collecting and archiving historical printing presses and typewriters. They also design, produce, and print everything from cards, stationery, and wedding invitations to fine packaging and book arts.

www.anonimaimpressori.it

BETTY SOLDI

Firenze, Italy

Calligrapher and designer descending from a Florentine family that has been handmaking fireworks since 1869, her studio and secret garden is located in the heart of Firenze.

www.bettysoldi.com

BONVINI 1909

Via Tagliamento, 1, Milano, Italy

Fratelli Bonvini stationery and typography shop, which opened its doors in 1909, is one of the oldest boutiques in Milano. It has been renovated and restored to its original beauty. The store offers vintage and contemporary writing tools, design stationery, letterpress services, workshops, a bookstore, and events related to typography, book arts, publishing, writing, and drawing.

www.bonvini1909.com

BOOKHOU

798 Dundas Street W, Toronto, Canada

A family-run multidisciplinary studio that emphasizes natural handmade materials and small production pieces.

www.bookhou.com

DONNA WILSON

17 Pundersons Gardens, Unit 8a, London, UK

Renowned for her distinctive use of color and pattern, Donna's designs are infused with her playful sense of humor, her love of nature, and a lifelong passion for craft and making.

www.donnawilson.com

KATIE LEAMON

Studio 28, The Trampery, 639 High Road, London, UK

Luxury cards, stationery, desk accessories, and wrapping paper, designed and made in the UK.

www.katieleamon.com

FOG LINEN WORK

5-35-1 Daita, Setagaya, Tokyo, Japan

Yumiko Sekine started her first business in 1993, importing used books and housewares from Europe and America to Japan. Now, Fog Linen Work is a lifestyle shop in Tokyo that specializes in linen products, both for the home and apparel.

www.foglinenwork.com

MARIA PICCI

Buenos Aires, Argentina

Maria designs and makes a textile jewelry line, made exclusively with our cotton ribbon, and she teaches workshops internationally.

www.mariapicci.com

OLA STUDIO

Bristol, England, UK

Makers of modern British stationery celebrating pattern and simplicity, Ola Studio is inspired by an appreciation of art, design, and craftsmanship.

www.olastudio.co.uk

RACHEL HAZELL

Isle of Iona, Scotland, UK

As a teacher, author, bookbinder, and traveler, words and the power of imagination have always been central to Rachel's life.

www.thetravellingbookbinder.com

TOLEMAIDE

Via Leonardo da Vinci 14, Bologna, Italy

Working from an eighteenth-century farmhouse near Bologna, Italy, Ethel Norcia has been designing and creating handcrafted jewelry for her celebrated brand, Tolemaide, since 2001.

www.tolemaide.com

UPPERCASE MAGAZINE

Calgary, Alberta, Canada

This quarterly magazine for the creative and curious is inspired by craft, design, typography, and illustration. Published by Janine Vangool since 2009.

www.uppercasemagazine.com

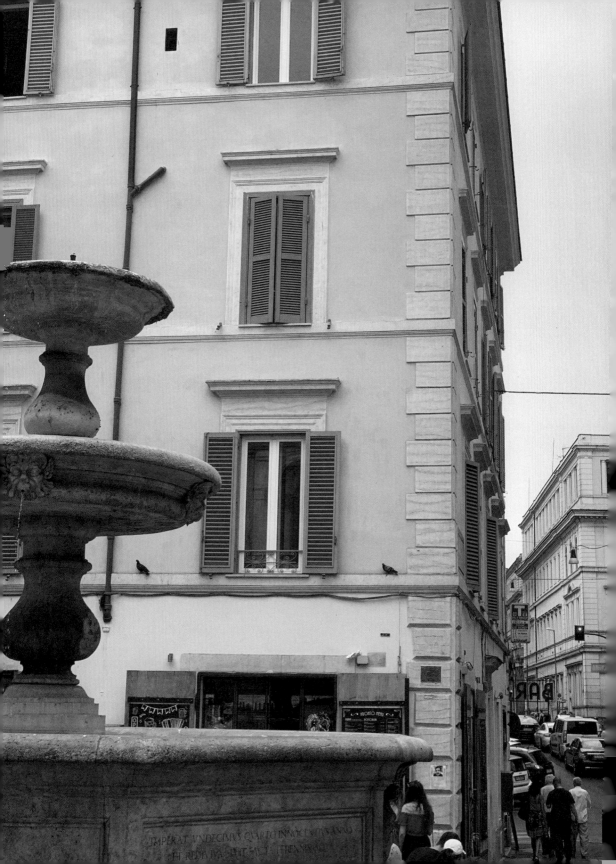

FAVORITES IN ROME

ANTICA CARTOTECNICA

Piazza dei Caprettari, 61

Established in 1930, Antica Cartotecnica carries a wide variety of calligraphy supplies, some from the 1930s and 1940s, including vintage nibs and ink, blank schoolbooks, and pencils.

www.anticacartotecnica.it

AZIENDA TESSILE ROMANA

Via San Nicola de' Cesarini, 13 (Largo Argentina)

Located in front of the ancient ruins of the sacred area of Largo Argentina, this historic textile company has been producing high-quality fabrics, curtains, and household linens since 1917.

www.aziendatessileromana.com

BOMBA

Via dell'Oca 39

A tailoring service and atelier founded by Cristina Bomba, making unique pieces with a beautiful selection of fabrics on display on the first floor. Bomba also carries clothing, lingerie, and accessories for men, women, and children in natural yarns, cashmere, silk, cotton, and linen. The shop itself is unique, with a sparse, simple display of beautiful textiles, a pleasure to the eye. Under historical vaults, there is a small water fountain to complement the interior. Since 2001, part of the space has been open for art and design exhibitions.

www.atelierbomba.com

CHEZ DEDE

Via di Monserrato, 35

Chez Dede is an independent brand and shop founded in 2011 by Andrea Ferolla and Daria Reina. With a French-Italian passport and an international audience, the shop features exclusive collections of accessories, fashion, home decor, and jewels.

www.chezdede.com

C.U.C.I.N.A.

Via Mario de' Fiori, 65

Just around the corner from the Spanish Steps, on a tiny street, you will find everything you love to have in your kitchen, from silverware and cups to moka machines and pasta makers to potholders and cotton and linen tea towels, all with a contemporary twist.

www.instagram.com/cucinastore/

DITTA G. POGGI

Via del Gesù, 74/75

Poggi is an art supply store, established in 1825, featuring a wide variety of art supplies, color pigments in old jars, and a quality selection of printing paper.

www.poggi1825.it

FABRIANO BOUTIQUE

Via del Babuino, 173

Fine stationery and modern paper design for blank and address books, folders, albums, pencils, and ink. Housed in a beautiful interior, based on old papermaking traditions, Fabriano Boutique carries products of minimal design on high quality paper.

www.fabrianoboutique.com

SILVANA AMATO AND EDIZIONI ALMENODUE

Rome, Italy

Silvana has been working for the past thirty years in publishing design and developing projects mainly in the cultural field. Under the imprint of Edizioni Almenodue, Angela and Silvana have collaborated with illustrators, calligraphers, printers, and type designers to produce a line of award-winning, limited-edition books and calendars.

www.silvanaamato.it

STAY

Via dei Falegnami, 63-64

Located in the traditional Jewish Quarter, well-known in Rome for textile and notions shops. The fine linen and homewares are designed by owners Rubel and Alessandra and exclusively made in Italy for their brand.

www.staystore.it

VERTECCHI

Via Della Croce, 70 a/b

An art supply store close to the Spanish Steps with a variety of office, graphic design, and art supplies, as well as wrapping and artist papers, boxes, stationery, fountain pens, and beautiful leather briefcases.

www.vertecchi.com

FOOD IN ROME

CAFFÈ DORIA

Via della Gatta, 1

Located in the courtyard of the historic Palazzo Doria Pamphilj, Caffè Doria is a bistro and cocktail bar within the museum. Galleria Doria Pamphilj is Rome largest private art collection, and the café, established in 1999, is a place to enjoy lunch or espresso in a beautiful setting.

www.anticocaffegreco.eu

CAFFÈ GRECO

Via dei Condotti, 86

Located just in front of the Spanish Steps since 1760, this centuries-old coffee house is where Lord Byron and Goethe had coffee, and also where Richard Wagner and Franz Liszt met for pastries. Its labyrinthine room conjures images of the past and the people that used to come here.

www.anticocaffegreco.eu

FORNO CAMPO DE' FIORI

Campo de' Fiori, 22

Angela has been coming here since age twelve, when her older brother brought her here on his motorcycle. For the best, always-fresh slice of pizza, go to this bakery! It also carries an unbelievable selection of bread, pastries, and cookies.

www.fornocampodefiori.com

GIOLITTI

Via degli Uffici del Vicario, 40

Giolitti has the fondest memories and the best gelato, featuring a wide variety of flavors, all exceptionally good. Located near the Parliament, it is in a beautiful area for strolling around with a gelato in your hands. It is also interesting to read the story of how it all began in 1890, and how they used to sell milk from their pastures in the Roman countryside.

www.giolitti.it

LA CASETTA A MONTI

Via della Madonna dei Monti, 62

This is a supercute café in Quartiere Monti; if you go, you will know why it has this name.

www.instagram.com/lacasettaamonti

LA QUERCIA OSTERIA MONTEFORTE

Piazza della Quercia, 23

Traditional Italian cuisine, in a small square, next to the church of Santa Maria della Quercia. Angela is particularly fond of this area of Rome, Rione Regola, where she used to walk, dream, and discover in her teen years. One of her favorite restaurants and favorite squares.

www.osterialaquercia.com

PANELLA

Via Merulana, 54

One of the best bakeries for breads of all shapes and tastes, fine pastries, chocolate, and pizza. Very close to one of the finest four basilicas of Rome: Santa Maria Maggiore. Off the major tourist area, it is an unforgettable bakery.

www.panellaroma.com

ROSCIOLI

Via dei Giubbonari, 21-22

La Salumeria Roscioli is a delicatessen, a pizzeria, a bakery, and a restaurant, where the cuisine is based on high-quality materials selected over the years by the Roscioli family.

www.salumeriaroscioli.com

SANT'EUSTACHIO IL CAFFÈ

Piazza Sant'Eustachio, 82

One of the best cafés in Rome is Sant'Eustachio, established in 1938, in Piazza Sant'Eustachio, 82, from which you can also see one of the most amazing baroque cupolas: Sant'Ivo alla Sapienza, by Francesco Borromini. The café has the most creamy, full-experience espresso, with authentic floor mosaics and interiors from the 1930s.

www.santeustachioilcaffe.it

SUPPLIZIO

Via dei Banchi Vecchi, 143

The taste of supplì, or fried rice balls with mozzarella in the middle, reminds Angela of the taste of childhood walks around Rome and a small snack before heading back home. Supplizio, in the Regola quarter, is a great place to sit in or outdoors for a quick taste of street food.

www.instagram.com/supplizioroma

TAZZA D'ORO

Via degli Orfani, 84

Right next to the Pantheon, in the same location since 1946, is Tazza d'Oro, for unforgettable granita di caffè con panna.

www.tazzadorocoffeeshop.com

MARKETS IN ROME

PORTA PORTESE

Porta Portese is the biggest and the most popular market in Rome, as Les Puces is in Paris and the Portobello Road is in London. Most anything can be found there: new and old clothes, shoes, leather goods, food, vintage, and antiques.

CAMPO DE' FIORI

The Campo de' Fiori flower and farmer market is one of the oldest in Rome, opening every morning since 1869. Beyond the daily market, the square is one of Rome's busiest and liveliest places, surrounded by shops, restaurants, and pubs.

FONTANELLA BORGHESE MARKET

The Fontanella Borghese Market, also known as Mercato delle Stampe, specializes in historic Italian prints and maps. It is located in the square just in front of Facoltà di Architettura, Università La Sapienza, in Piazza Fontanella Borghese. The market is small and quiet, in a beautiful, intimate square.

MERCATO DI VIA TITO SPERI

Mercato di via Tito Speri, in Piazza Mazzini, is Angela's favorite market for finding fresh fruits and veggies, baked goods, and even vintage textiles. The market is well known and attended by people in Prati, the area where she grew up, and where she returns every time she is in Rome.

Photography Credits

Principal photography by Dane Tashima

Additional photography by:

Lily Reid: pages 5 (third from left), 124, 126–29

Bari Zaki: pages 8 (left), 10 (third from left)

Laura Shelby Murphy: pages 10 (top, second from left), 14, 15, 18, 19, 72, 114–19

Nadá Alaeddin: pages 10 (top, center), 154 (top)

Angela Liguori: pages 10 (bottom left), 16, 17, 20–23, 32, 33, 98–115, 132, 136–45, 148–55, 156 (second row following), 170–75

Justine Hand: pages 28, 29, 157

Maria Picci: pages 120, 122, 123

Brian Doben: page 147

Acknowledgments

There are so many wonderful people to thank. A village of many makes Studio Carta possible, and others have made this book—a longtime dream of mine—possible.

The deepest thanks to my family: my parents, who were my inspiration to launch Studio Carta. My mother, who was a seamstress her whole life, and my father are with me always. Mohamed, my partner in life and business: thank you for managing the behind-the-scenes of Studio Carta—from logistics, to packing, to building, to espresso making, you do it all with a smile. My children, Nadá, Hani, and Nael, our motivations for working hard each day: you make Studio Carta a true and special family business. I am so proud of our family team.

Thank you to our talented producer, Jan Hartman of Jan Hartman Books, who created the idea for this book and edited the content, and the expert team at Abrams: Shawna Mullen, Brooke Reynolds, Jenice Kim, Logan Hill, and Kathleen Gaffney. Coco McCracken, thank you for capturing my story with your lovely words. Dane Tashima, your photographs are ones I will cherish always. Laura Murphy and Silke Stoddard, it all started with your imaginations and support from the very first order of ribbon for *Martha Stewart Living*—thank you for being inspired by Studio Carta ribbon, and for creating endless beauty with it.

To the people who make our wholesale and retail business run smoothly, our incredible clients and stockists, and Studio Carta employees past and present: you help to grow our business and make each day more creative. Thank you.

To our unmatched Studio Carta community: your passion for our products, events, and partnerships and your encouragement along the way have made being in this business such a pleasure. Thank you for inspiring us—for visiting us and liking, sharing, and following us on this journey.

Studio Carta has never just been a store for me. It's a far-reaching community, a collaborative physical and figurative space to share ideas and connect over making beautiful things. Together.

Thank you.